# WOMEN WHO EMBEZZLE OR DEFRAUD

PRAEGER SPECIAL STUDIES IN SOCIAL WELFARE

GENERAL EDITORS:

*Neil Gilbert and*
*Harry Specht*

# WOMEN WHO EMBEZZLE OR DEFRAUD

## A Study of Convicted Felons

*Dorothy Zietz*

PRAEGER

PRAEGER SPECIAL STUDIES • PRAEGER SCIENTIFIC

**Library of Congress Cataloging in Publication Data**

Zietz, Dorothy.
Women who embezzle or defraud.

(Praeger special studies in social welfare)
Includes bibliographical references and index.
1. Female offenders—United States. 2. Fraud—United States
3. Embezzlement—United States. I. Title.
II. Series.
HV6791.Z49 364.1'62'0973 81-8638
ISBN 0-03-059592-4 AACR2

Published in 1981 by Praeger Publishers
CBS Educational and Professional Publishing
A Division of CBS, Inc.
521 Fifth Avenue, New York, New York 10175 U.S.A.



123456789 145 987654321

Printed in the United States of America

# FOREWORD

## *Vernon Fox*

Women have been neglected by criminologists because they so seldom appear in the criminal justice system. They comprise about 16 percent of all arrests and about 5 percent of the prison population. Ma Barker was considered by J. Edgar Hoover to have been the most dangerous female criminal in American history, but she was never apprehended. When Gustav de Beaumont and Alexis de Tocqueville wrote their famous On the Penitentiary System of the United States and Its Application in France, published in 1833, they reported that women made up 4 percent of the prison population. The women's liberation movement apparently has not had much impact on female crime, since the current total prison population includes only slightly more than 5 percent females. Consequently, most studies of criminal behavior and typologies have been with men.

Dr. Zietz has made a pioneering study by focusing upon the typology of female crime. She compares females convicted of embezzlement and fraud with a typology of male embezzlers reported in Cressey's Other People's Money, published in 1953, and finds that "women are different." In fact, typologies developed by other writers do not appear to be wholly applicable to women. The vocabularies of adjustment are very different from those by which men justify their crimes. Female crime more frequently involves an emotional relationship with others, generally children or men, with the concept of role fulfillment. Only a few, whom Dr. Zietz calls Greedy Opportunists, experience an erosion of values.

This enlightening study of the typologies of females who embezzle and defraud furnishes an understanding of women who commit crime not heretofore available. Dr. Zietz has made a valuable contribution to criminology. She has opened new vistas that define the sex roles in society through criminal behavior.

# PREFACE

This book has a five-part purpose: to review the literature as it pertains to women who commit property offenses; to examine concepts and typologies that seem to have some relevance to the behavior of women who embezzle or defraud and, at later points, to assess the applicability of these constructs to women who commit such offenses; to explore, in depth, the similarities and differences in the findings in Cressey's study of men who violated financial trust and in my study of women who met Cressey's criteria for inclusion in his study; to describe the characteristics and behavior of a group of incarcerated women who intended to steal or defraud; and to encourage further research to test the validity of the tentative typology developed to provide a basis for classification of the behavior systems of women who embezzle or defraud.

The act of embezzlement is usually considered to involve a situation in which a person who was legally employed to deal with public or private monies, goods, or property subsequently violates, intentionally and willfully, the trust inherent in such employment. The law submits that the offender first had the opportunity and then the intent to appropriate illegally such funds or other property for personal gain. In cases of embezzlement, apprehension usually follows detection because of the readily available tangible evidence that audits and law enforcement techniques can reveal. The fact of fraud, on the other hand, places the offender and the victim in much more ambiguous positions and allows for greater opportunity to engage in a wide variety of petty or gross illegal operations. Each of these crimes, however, has certain elements of subjective judgment since individual state penal codes often make no clear distinction between the crimes of embezzlement and fraud. The codes tend to overlap and generally define embezzlement and fraud interchangeably, describing both offenses as being: an intentional perversion of truth; the false representation of fact by word and action; the offering of false or misleading allegations or terms of contract; the concealment of information that should be disclosed; and the intentional misrepresentation of fact.

Although there are some rather clear similarities between embezzlement and fraud, there are significant differences. The embezzler is likely to have sustained periods of time in which to engage in criminal activities. The embezzler may indeed be protected by the sheer complexity of a highly personalized accounting system and by status as an established and trustworthy employee or private businessperson. The person practicing fraud, however, is supported in criminal activities primarily by personal persuasiveness and by reluctance of the victim to admit gullibility. However, the tricks of the trade are more easily identifiable than are the psychosocial factors involved in these two widely prevalent types of crime.

This study of female embezzlement and fraud was made at the California Institution for Women. It supports the thesis that these offenses do not reflect a homogeneous class of criminal behavior since some women were sentenced for an offense that was not consistent with the legal definition of the criminal act, and others who were embezzlers were sentenced for something else.

I must acknowledge here my indebtedness to the people who made this study possible. My first thanks must go to the California Department of Corrections, whose director made it possible for me to become a temporary employee of the department during the first phase of the study. I am particularly indebted to the superintendents of the California Institution for Women for their cooperation and assistance. I am also grateful to members of the staff at CIW for their acceptance of my role and their help in arranging interviews with inmates, and in contributing ideas as the study progressed. I also wish to thank the women interviewed, particularly those whose case histories are summarized. Names of all persons and business organizations are fictional.

I owe a very special thanks to Professor Donald R. Cressey for his gracious permission to quote extensively from his impressive pioneering work on the study of embezzlement. I acknowledge, too, with much gratitude, the contributions made by colleagues who read the manuscript and made valuable suggestions for its expansion and final format. However, I must assume sole responsibility for the content.

My deepest appreciation is extended to Dorothy M. Kurtz, whose patient suggestions made the editorial chores less difficult, and to Carol Larsen, who provided excellent assistance in editing and typing the manuscript. Finally, I am deeply grateful to Lynda Sharp, editor, whose perceptive reading of the manuscript helped to place the contents into useful sequence.

# CONTENTS

# I

# INTRODUCTION

# 1

# HISTORICAL PERSPECTIVES

This book was initially designed to determine whether the generalizations presented by Cressey in his classic study of male embezzlement would have equal validity for a comparable group of women incarcerated at the California Institution for Women (CIW). To test other hypotheses, CIW residents who did not meet Cressey's primary criterion ("the person . . . accepted a position of trust in good faith"(1)) were retained in this study. A representative group of women convicted of forgery was subsequently added to the original sample. A more detailed description of the methodology used in this book will be presented after a review of its historical and conceptual base.

## AN OVERVIEW

Study of the criminal behavior of women has been characterized by intermittent thrusts of activity, strange avoidances, and prevalent assumptions that: sex differentials are not significant in the construction of typologies or in theory building; any attempt to examine the criminal behavior of women would be meaningless because of the small samples available; and because, with certain bizarre exceptions, "female crime mainly follows the dull pattern of drunkenness, vagrancy, prostitution, disorderly conduct, drug addiction, and the like."(2)

To some extent these attitudes seem evident in sequential time frames. At several points a well-conceived study of female offenders has been followed by apparent indifference to the data produced. In more recent years the development of typologies that make no reference to women might be attributed to the study site selected by a particular investigator, such as, a male correctional institution. In any event, it seems pertinent to review briefly the developmental history of research relating to the criminal behavior of women.

## EARLY YEARS OF THIS CENTURY

Criminology texts customarily trace the ideological development of that discipline from the eighteenth century, with early reference to the work of Lombroso and the Italian or positivistic school. Several pages are usually devoted to a review of Lombroso's notions as expressed in his initial work and in "the numerous subsequent editions" of that publication.(3) Walter Reckless(4) seems almost unique in his awareness of the fact that Lombroso and Ferrero also published The Female Offender in 1900. The typology presented in that study included the concept of the "occasional offender,"(5) later described by Ruth Cavan(6) and more recently by Clinard and Quinney.(7)

During the first four decades of this century, sporadic efforts to identify and/or describe the characteristics and behavior of women convicted of crime were made by at least three groups. Several intensive research studies provided a wide range of data about the mental, physical, and social attributes of women offenders in New York,(8) Massachusetts,(9) and several other states.(10) Newspapers and periodicals chronicled the feats of women who had committed crimes involving multiple murders, kidnapping, or the illegal acquisition of large sums of money.(11) In addition, several books were written by former wardens of prisons for women.(12) As Mabel Elliott stated at a later date, their accounts also tended to describe spectacular rather than typical cases(13) and to contain "more information about the warden than her charges."(14) These developments are important primarily because of what happened next.

## THE MIDDLE YEARS

In the next era, an increasing number of authors began to deplore the paucity of research on the criminal behavior of women. Thorsten Sellin, Reckless, and Barnes and Teeters are of particular interest because their concern produced results relevant to this study. Sellin appears to have inspired Otto Pollak to undertake the monumental task of presenting, under the title The Criminality of Women, an "integrated analysis of the major conjectures and research findings so far available in the American, English, French, German literature [ with ] some references . . . to Italian, Dutch and South American material."(15) The bibliography he compiled(16) is a valuable contributions to any study of law violation by women. Unfortunately, the content of his work was marred by an apparent need to validate, beyond the shadow of a doubt, his belief that "the amount of female crime has been greatly underestimated by traditional opinion,"(17) and that this can be attributed to the fact that women are more deceitful than men.(18) Some of the premises on which he based these conclusions will have value as we examine and seek to understand the ways in which theorists and textbook authors have ignored or presented the fact that women do commit crimes.

Reckless responded to the publication of Pollak's book by including in the third edition of his text a chapter of the same name ("The Criminality of Women")(19) in which he reviewed, in some detail, the contributions of Lombroso and Pollak. More significantly, a prior section explained his belief that "the criminality of women should be considered a special order of criminal behavior" because it has "its own specifics just as there are specifics about white collar crimes, ordinary criminal careers and so forth."(20) His rationale for this strange exclusion of women from consideration under other specific orders of criminal behavior is explained in the following conclusion: "If the criminologist, before propounding or accepting any theory of crime and delinquency, would pause to ask whether that theory applied to women, he would probably discard it because of its inapplicability to women."(21)

Barnes and Teeters also used Pollak's title for a section of the 1959 edition of their text, and included in its content a brief summary of Pollak's conclusions.(22) In this section they presented a catchall grouping of women criminals who are "calculating, fascinating and intelligent, who capitalize on their charm and femininity,"(23) and those who follow "the dull pattern" of female crime. In earlier sections of this chapter, however, reference is made to "men and women [who] are in our prisons for the first time and for their first offense" and "who may be referred to as situational criminals"(24) and to the "suave confidence man or woman, check passer or forger [who] is a traditional criminal."(25) Reference to "a confidence woman" is of particular interest because more recent authors, like Roebuck and Blum, devote whole chapters to the behavior of the confidence man with no indication that women might engage in similar "games,"(26) or with only a terse acknowledgment that one or more women were included in the sample studied.(27)

Elliott's response to Pollak's study provides an interesting variation. Like Reckless, she discussed in separate chapters "The Woman Offender" and "The Types of Women Who Break the Law,"(28) and included in her presentation a summary of Pollak's major theses. Unlike Reckless and Barnes and Teeters, she did not regard Pollak's work as a major contribution in meeting the "real need for definitive research . . . on the criminal activities of women." Instead, she contended that he "provides very little truly scientific material" and gives "a liberal subjective interpretation" to his data in an effort "to shatter the notion that women are less criminal than men" and, because they are deceitful, "merely conceal their crimes more frequently than do men."(29) She explained in logical fashion her reasons for believing that many of Pollak's conclusions were fallacious or equally applicable to male criminals, and then proceeded to outline her belief that "the disparity in crime rates of men and women seems rather to lie in the special characteristics of their respective cultures."(30) It will be important to acknowledge the relevance of this concept as we examine the motivation of women who violate positions of trust. For our present purposes it is more appropriate to note the strange dichotomy she perpetuated by: first, synthesizing in two chapters data selected to prove her thesis that "women commit a wide variety of crimes"; and second, omitting any reference to women in the preceding chapters describing "the major types of offenders" and "the professional criminal and organized crime." This conceptual segregation is perhaps most evident in the former chapter, in which an early statement reads: "We need to keep in mind that criminals are men – men with families and friends, men out of work and ill advised, . . . greedy men, men in the depths of economic despair, men with false ambitions."(31) A few pages later she introduced a section on "Embezzlers" by stating: "The men who embezzle yield to what is a very easy temptation,"(32) with no indication that her subsequent chapter on "The Types of Women Who Break the Law" would contain a section on "Economic Offenders" devoted primarily to a discussion of female embezzlers.

Thus four authors, aware of Pollak's work, elected to follow his example in describing separately the criminal behavior of women. It is interesting to note, however, that none of them (or any other authors reviewed) makes any reference to the ideas expressed by Pollak in introducing his final "Summary":

> In our male-dominated culture, women have always been considered strange. . . . Suppressing them and needing them at the same time, men have never been completely comfortable in their apparent state of social superiority and have always been apprehensive of the possibility of rebellion or revenge on the part of women. . . . Basically they have attempted to deny women the ability to do things and have either idealized them into a sweetness and purity which made them appear docile and harmless, or they have maligned them in order to be able to condemn them. Both types of behavior help men to feel better about their denial of equality to women. Thus, many male attempts to understand women have actually been attempts to rationalize men's treatment of the other sex and have frequently been nothing but self deceptions.(33)

Pollak used this paragraph to explain the reason he felt it important "to collect and analyze the available information regarding female crime."(34) For us it may explain the continuing omission of any reference to women in most efforts to develop classifications, typologies, and theories to further our understanding of criminal behavior.

## MORE RECENT DEVELOPMENTS

It would be erroneous to leave the impression that no research has been completed on the behavior of female law violators since 1950. On the contrary, an exploratory study conducted at the California Institution for Women by this investigator(35) was followed by a more extensive research effort to identify the service needs of families while the mothers were incarcerated in that institution, and to discover existing obstacles to meeting these needs in the community and in the institution.(36) In 1964 a study of homosexuality as a mode of adaptation in a women's prison was made in the same institution.(37) Ruth Glick's 1977 study of women's correctional programs represents the most comprehensive examination of women in jails and state prisons.(38) Conceptually, however, other studies have greater relevance to this study.

Widespread concern about child abuse prompted Leontine Young,(39) David Gil,(40) Vincent de Francis,(41) Serapio Zalba,(42) and others to undertake extensive research on the criminal behavior of abusing parents and/or attempt the construction of typologies based on two-sex role behaviors. In more recent years, Dale Hoffman-Bustamante's study of the nature of female criminality documented important sex differences in role expectations, socialization patterns, and opportunities to commit particular offenses.(43) Rose Giallombardo's earlier study of the social organization of the Federal Reformatory for Women at Alderson, West Virginia, seems to have a more specific value. It was designed to examine, in an exploratory way, the structure of a women's prison as an organization of roles and functions,(44) and to compare the findings with the literature on the male prison. This approach would seem to hold particular promise for future research and theory building because it offers an opportunity for valid comparison of the criminal behavior of men and women who are readily available for study. To date, there has been no comparable effort to determine whether or not typologies and theories relating to the behavior of male offenders against property are equally valid when applied to women who commit similar offenses.

## NOTES

(1) Donald R. Cressey, A Study in the Social Psychology of Embezzlement: Other People's Money (Glencoe, Ill.: Free Press, 1953), p. 20.

(2) Harry Elmer Barnes and Negley K. Teeters, New Horizons in Criminology, 3rd ed. (Englewood Cliffs, N.J.: Prentice-Hall, 1959), p. 64.

(3) Herbert A. Bloch and Gilbert Geis, Men, Crime and Society (New York: Random House, 1962), p. 89.

(4) Walter C. Reckless, The Crime Problem, 3rd ed. (New York: Appleton-Century-Crofts, 1961), pp. 79-82.

(5) Cesare Lombroso and William Ferrero, The Female Offender (New York: Appleton, 1900), pp. 192-216.

(6) Ruth Shonle Cavan, Criminology (New York: Crowell, 1948), pp. 183-93.

(7) Marshal B. Clinard and Richard Quinney, Criminal Behavior Systems, A Typology, 2nd ed. (New York: Holt, Rinehart and Winston, 1973), pp. 57-77.

(8) Mabel R. Fernald, Mary Holmes Stevens Hayes, and Almena Dawley, A Study of Women Delinquents in New York State (New York: Century, 1920).

(9) Sheldon and Eleanor Glueck, 500 Delinquent Women (New York: Knopf, 1934).

(10) Edith R. Spaulding, "The Results of Mental and Physical Examinations of 400 Women Offenders – with Particular Reference to Their Treatment During Commitment," Journal of the American Institute of Criminal Law and Criminology (1914-15): 704-17.

(11) Barnes and Teeters, New Horizons, pp. 62-64.

(12) Mary B. Harris, I Knew Them in Prison (New York: Viking, 1936); and Florence Monahan, Women in Crime (New York: Ives Washburn, 1941).

(13) Mabel A. Elliott, Crime in Modern Society (New York: Harper & Brothers, 1952), p. 228.

(14) Ibid., p. 255.

(15) Otto Pollak, The Criminality of Women (New York: Barnes, 1950), p. xv.

(16) Ibid., pp. 162-75.

(17) Ibid., p. 161.

(18) Ibid., p. 8.

(19) Reckless, Crime Problem, pp. 78-96.

(20) Ibid., p. 78.

(21) Ibid.

(22) Barnes and Teeters, New Horizons, p. 62.

(23) Ibid.

(24) Ibid., p. 53.

(25) Ibid., p. 51.

(26) Julian B. Roebuck, Criminal Typology (Springfield, Ill.: Charles C. Thomas, 1967), pp. 182-201.

(27) Richard H. Blum, Deceivers and Deceived (Springfield, Ill.: Charles C. Thomas, 1972), pp. 12-60.

(28) Elliott, Crime in Modern Society, pp. 199-255.

(29) Ibid., p. 199.

(30) Ibid., p. 201.

(31) Ibid., p. 102.

(32) Ibid., p. 109.

(33) Pollak, Criminality of Women, p. 149.

(34) Ibid.

(35) Dorothy Zietz, "Child Welfare Services in a Women's Correctional Institution," Child Welfare 42 (April 1963).

(36) Serapio R. Zalba, Women Prisoners and Their Families (Sacramento: California Department of Social Welfare and California Department of Corrections, 1964).

(37) David A. Ward and Gene G. Kassebaum, "Homosexuality: A Mode of Adaptation in a Prison for Women," Social Problems 12 (1964): 159-77.

(38) Ruth M. Glick, National Study of Women's Correctional Programs (Washington, D.C.: Government Printing Office, 1977).

(39) Leontine Young, Wednesday's Children (New York: McGraw-Hill, 1964).

(40) David Gil, Violence Against Children: Physical Child Abuse in the United States (Cambridge: Harvard University Press, 1970).

(41) Vincent de Francis, Child Abuse: Preview of a Nationwide Survey (Denver: American Humane Association, Children's Division, 1963).

(42) Serapio R. Zalba, "The Abused Child: A Survey of the Problem," Social Work 11 (October 1966): 3-16, and 12 (January 1967): 70-79.

(43) Dale Hoffman-Bustamante, "The Nature of Female Criminality," Issues in Criminology 8 (Fall 1973): 117.

(44) Rose Giallombardo, Society of Women: A Study of a Women's Prison (New York: Wiley, 1966).

# 2

# RELEVANT STUDIES AND TYPOLOGIES

Each year publishers' listings grow longer as authors with varying professional backgrounds add new data and new ideas to the existing knowledge of criminal behavior. It would not be appropriate to attempt to review here more than a representative sample of research findings, typologies, and bits of theory that might have relevance to this study. It does seem essential, however, to examine some of the general considerations that provided a conceptual framework for the methodology to be described in the next chapter.

Criminologists agree that the "earliest and still the most common way of classifying criminals is in terms of the legal title identifying the criminal act."(1) There is also general agreement with Reckless's contention that "the convenient legal labels for crimes in the criminal code are not adequate behavioral descriptions."(2) In listing the disadvantages or limitations of this method of classification, mention is usually made of the facts that: a legal category tells nothing about the person or his situation; labeling the offender by his act creates an erroneous impression that criminals commit only one type of crime and are the product of a similar developmental process; the legal definitions of a crime are very different in the various states; and the practice of plea bargaining or pleading guilty to a lesser charge in expectation of a minimum penalty may result in wide disparity between the criminal act and the crime on which conviction was based.(3)

As Clinard and Quinney pointed out, there have been numerous efforts "to overcome some of the problems of legalistic classifications, while still utilizing the legal categories."(4) Some theorists have elected to use a general legal category such as "crimes against property," with subtypes based on the mode of operation,(5) the pattern of arrest records,(6) or some combination of legal offense with offender characteristics (for example, amateur shoplifter, professional thief, and so on).(7) Others, like Reimer and Lemert, focused their research on specific crimes and developed subtypes reflecting the circumstances under which the crime is likely to occur(8) and/or the usual characteristics of persons who commit this crime (such as "the native check forger"(9) and "the systematic check forger"(10)). Another group approached the problem from the opposite direction. They grouped together several legal categories in an effort to identify a process that must precede the commission of a criminal act(11) or form a sociological unit that could be used in describing "a homogeneous class of behavior."(12) This approach is best illustrated by Cressey's decision to select for study male inmates whose behavior constituted "criminal violation of financial trust," even though they may have been convicted of embezzlement, forgery, confidence, and/or larceny by bailee.(13) His methodology and conclusions will be discussed more fully as relevant findings in this study are presented in Chapter 5.

In an effort to pull together some of the other ways in which classifications have been constructed, Korn and McCorkle established three categories that are useful in considering an array of different theoretical approaches.

## CLASSIFICATION BY TYPE OF PERSON

Korn and McCorkle included in the category of type of person only the classifications based on "hereditary physical type" (for example, Lombroso's "born criminal" and Hooton's "constitutional defective") and on "psychological type or condition or disease." They believed this approach shared many of the limitations of classification by legal category because it ignores situational factors as causal elements, may produce rigid diagnostic categories, and may create the false impression that similar personality types commit similar offenses.(14) In a subsequent chapter, these authors reviewed the "genetic, glandular and constitutional theories of crime," including Lombroso's evolving conceptions, but made no mention of the fact that Lombroso considered the female offender a special type with three or more subtypes. First is "the born criminal – whose criminal propensities are more intense and more perverse than those of their male prototypes,"(15) and may lead to offenses in which "vengeance plays a principal part"(16) or "greed is a moving cause".(17) Second is the "occasional criminal," for whom "in many cases, the origin of her reluctant crime . . . is suggestion on the part of a lover, or sometimes of her father or brother,"(18) or in cases of "offenses against property . . . committed by normal or nearly normal women . . . a sheer excess of temptation."(19) The final group, which has little relevance to this study, includes "criminal female lunatics, women who commit crimes of passion."(20)

Korn and McCorkle concluded: "Research in the relationship between crime and physical factors has not only failed to reveal any causal link but has failed to produce evidence of any association whatever." They hastened to add, however, that this "does not imply that physical factors have no relationship with criminal behavior."(21)

More recent texts review the continuing efforts to locate the causes of crime and mental illness in some internal biological defect, such as an abnormal chromosomal pattern (XYY) or a biochemical deficiency associated with schizophrenia. Despite the negative or inconclusive results of this type of single-factor research, it has become apparent that certain physical factors do assume important roles in determining human behavior. Several studies of a very different order have shown that a factor of "physical attractiveness" customarily plays a significant part in determining the response of parents, family, friends, and teachers to children; the grades a child will receive in school; his interaction with his peers and consequently the self-image he will develop and the vocational or professional opportunities that will become available to him.(22) Any attempt to identify physical attractiveness or the lack of it as a primary cause of crime would ignore all current knowledge of multiple causation; however, personal appearance and manner may well determine, in part, the opportunity to commit certain kinds of offenses and the option a frustrated or desperate person might select in efforts to solve an existing problem.

To Korn and McCorkle, a woman is not a "type of person." In fact, the word "women" does not appear in their index even though some information about sex ratios in different offenses is provided in their chapter on "The Data of Criminology."(23) Unlike Reckless (whom they quote in other connections), they did not include women in their chapter on "Special Offender Categories." Instead, they described under this title "offenses that are dealt with by special judicial and administrative procedures" (such as sex offenders and drug offenders).(24)

As indicated in the previous chapter, Pollak did consider women "a type of person," and saw his approach as requiring an investigation of "(1) the ways in which women commit their crimes, (2) the amount of female criminality . . . (3) the specificity of female crime, (4) the personal characteristics of female offenders, and (5) the factors of causation which distinguish women criminals from other offender groups."(25) Most of his conclusions have no specific relevance to this study, but it is of interest to note his conviction that "the specificity of female crime has to be looked for rather in method and in procedure than in the interest violated by certain offense categories,"(26) and that "meaningful differentials between male and female crime must be looked for . . . in the ways in which women commit their crimes and in the causes of their criminal behavior."(27)

## CLASSIFICATION BY LIFE ORGANIZATION

In presenting the classification by life organization, Korn and McCorkle explained: "For some offenders crime is a career and a livelihood; for others, a single, never-to-be-repeated outburst; for still others a recurring alternative."(28) They credited the European criminologists Mayhew and Moreau with proposing a system of classification that related crime to other life activities, and identified the categories of "professional offender," "accidental offender," and "habitual offender." Korn and McCorkle also described, at some length, the modifications made in this category by Lindesmith and Dunham, who conceptualized a "continuum of socialization" ranging from the completely socialized criminal to the "individualized offender." Although they believed this system had advantages over classification by type of legal offense or type of person, they concluded that it involved an excessive condensation of concepts and is "more a theory of crime causation than a method of classification."(29)

As indicated in the preceding chapter, Elliott expressed her conviction that "men and women live in different worlds" and that some of the crimes women commit grow out of the culture of their private world. She supported this conclusion by citing evidence that women often commit crimes to protect or promote a life organization in which a child or husband plays a central role. In her words:

> The driving motivations in the average woman's life tend to be emotional. . . . The concentration of interest in her family's welfare results in a peculiar type of emotional selfishness. She is primarily concerned about <u>her</u> family, <u>her</u> husband, <u>her</u> children, <u>her</u> home. . . . Emotional security tends to be her major aim and highest goal.(30)

Although this conclusion may be overstated as a generalization, it represents a factor to be examined in any study of female criminal behavior.

Concepts and classifications presented by Mayhew, Sutherland, Cavan, Gibbons, Abrahamson, Guttmacher, and others reflect an awareness that a positive or negative relationship may exist between the criminal act of an offender and his life organization. Gibbons refers to "situational factors in criminality" and explains that "law-breaking behavior may arise out of some combination of situational pressures and circumstances, along with opportunities for criminality which are totally outside the actors."(31) This concept is evident in his chapter entitled "Criminality among 'Respectable Citizens,' " in which he discusses embezzlers, reviews the studies of Cressey and others, and comments again on his belief that inadequate attention has been paid "to situational contexts that may contribute to trust violation."(32) Cavan presented a similar thrust as she discussed "criminals who live in a non-criminal world."(33) She explained that these are"persons who do not regard themselves as criminals nor as opposed to conventional moral codes,"(34) and included in this category: "the occasional offender," who may accompany companions on a burglary without much consideration of the nature of his act, or who may embezzle funds to maintain a life organization that is threatened, avoid a painful situation, or meet an immediate need; and the "episodic offender," described as a special type of occasional offender who commits a criminal act under the stress of a particular set of circumstances or temptation that probably will not recur, and who receives no lasting satisfaction from his act (such as an embezzler with a sudden need for money he cannot obtain in a legitimate way).(35)

The concept of the occasional offender, introduced by Lombroso, continues to appear in various typologies and may or may not show a direct relation to the concept of life organization. In most instances, the author's definition of the term indicates clearly that it refers only incidentally to the absence of repetitive criminal acts, and instead emphasizes the offender's self-concept as a noncriminal, the conformity of his value system with that of law-abiding persons, and the disparity between his life organization and his criminal act.

In discussing "traditional crime," Barnes and Teeters use the term occasional offender as a synonym for the "situational criminal" as differentiated from the "chronic offender."(36) Clinard and Quinney are more specific in listing "occasional property criminal behavior" as one of the nine types of criminal behavior they identified, but omit from this category embezzlement and other violations of trust, which they classify as "occupational criminal behavior." They attribute to both types, however, "a life organization . . . not built around a criminal role."(37) Gibbons creates another kind of dichotomy when he describes nine types of "property offender careers" and lists separately three types that engage in "professional theft as a way of life," and four types of offenders who do not define themselves as lawbreakers, including the "naive check forger" and the "one-time loser." As previously stated, he excludes from the latter category the embezzler, whom he classifies as an example of one type of "criminality among respectable citizens."(38)

Mayhew's concept of the "accidental offender" also survives, with varying meanings. As originally presented, this category included all persons who did not earn a living through crime and who became law violators through the pressure of unanticipated circumstances. Manfred S. Guttmacher continued to use the term as an equivalent of the "occasional criminal" who is pressured into a criminal act by a special set of circumstances.(39) Conversely, David Abrahamson developed a more precise typology that differentiated the "chronic offender" from the "acute criminal" and subdivided the latter category into: the "situational offender" who acts on the basis of opportunity and need; the "associational offender" who is influenced by the antisocial behavior patterns of his family or friends; and the "accidental offender" who commits a crime without intent, such as a traffic accident caused by negligent driving, or property damage resulting from the careless disposition of a burning match.(40)

Another approach to the relationship between criminal behavior and life-style or organization can be found in Sutherland's concept of white-collar crime. As he originally defined this term in 1939, it referred to "crime in the upper or white collar class, composed of respectable or at least respected business and professional men."(41) At some subsequent point, he modified the meaning of the term by stating that "white collar crime may be defined approximately as a crime committed by a person of respectability and high status in the course of his occupation."(42) In a later definition he appeared to exclude embezzlement and other crimes against employers: "The white collar criminal is defined as a person with high socio-economic status who violates the laws designed to regulate his occupational activities."(43)

These changing and imprecise definitions have led to differences of opinion that criminologists have resolved in various ways. Bloch and Geis concluded that the category had become so suffused with controversy that it would be desirable to consider separately

> those white collar crimes committed (a) by individuals as individuals (e.g., lawyers, doctors), (b) by employees against the corporation (e.g., embezzlers), and (c) by policy-making officials for the corporation (as, for example, in the recent anti-trust cases).(44)

Gibbons resolved the dilemma more decisively by simply proclaiming his intent to reserve the term "for violations of business regulations or occupational roles carried on as contradictory to the business or occupational enterprise."(45) As previously indicated, he considers embezzlement to be a separate type of "criminality among respectable citizens" and defends this segregation by stating: "Embezzlers are 'enemies within' who surreptitiously steal the assets of the organization and make no contribution to the economic health of the business concern."(46) Akers solves the problem in another way by: following Quinney's example in equating white-collar crime to "occupational crime"; defining it as "violations of legal norms governing lawful occupational endeavors during the course of practicing the occupation"; and severing the tie between the criminal act and the offender's social status or other life activities through a definition that refers to a violation that occurs "as part of, or a deviation from, the violator's occupational role – whether it is blue collar or white collar or lower class or upper class."(47)

## CLASSIFICATION BY CRIMINAL CAREER

In defining his concept of a criminal career, Reckless stipulated that its four basic components include: involvement in crimes of gain, usually offenses against property; a scheme of life in which certain criminal activities are elected as an occupation and major economic support is derived from them; the progressive development of certain skills and techniques that are often specialized in nature, while the offender maintains some association with other career criminals and develops attitudes favorable to continuation in crime with little concern about the moral aspects of his behavior; and the absence of "any strong, impelling mental components such as a compulsion or an excessive immaturity."(48) Reckless excludes from consideration as career criminals the habitual offenders "who are driven by strong mental components" and have not been involved in "socially processed careers that are the products of a certain line of social experience."(49)

The terms "criminal careers" and "career criminals" have particular relevance to the findings in this study. Before reviewing the development and current use of the underlying concept, it may be useful to examine some of the notions of what it does not include, and what ideational disposition has been made of excluded patterns of criminal behavior as they relate to property offenses.

Reckless's concept of "the habitual offender" is not unique. It seems to approximate Moreau's definition of the same term that he adopted to supplement Mayhew's categories ("the professional offender" and "the accidental offender") because he believed they did not describe the large class of offenders who are deficient in intelligence and self-control, and therefore yield easily to impulse whenever pressured by temptation or circumstance.(50) Reckless, however, did not classify the activities of the habitual offender as one of the "specific orders of criminal behavior," and did not define the term in any precise way. In efforts to clarify his concept of the criminal career, he merely made evident his intent to exclude

> habitual drunkards who have made many appearances in police courts . . . and jails, [sex offenders], drug addicts who . . . have no specialized form of theft . . . developed to maintain the habit, . . . recidivists, and habitual offenders who are driven by strong mental components to repeat in crime and to relapse time after time.(51)

Cavan presented "the habitual offender" in a separate chapter with that title and described, as subtypes, drunkards, drug addicts, vagrants, petty thieves, and criminal vendors (for example, "the small drug peddler, the semi-professional prostitute or streetwalker, and those who offer gambling devices in violation of the law"(52)). She defined "the habitual criminal" as one whose offenses are "either habits in the literal sense of the word, which have been made illegal, or they are crimes in the common acceptance of the term, repeatedly but not skillfully performed."(53) At a later point, she reemphasized the dichotomy implied in this definition by stating:

> In addition to the habitual offenders who shade off into personally disorganized and socially maladjusted types, there are the habitual offenders who stand midway between the occasional offender and the professional criminal. These men and women are usually thieves of some sort or they cater to desires of others that cannot be satisfied legally. In the case of petty thieves . . . they are amateurs both in executing the crime and in disposing of the goods. Consequently, they are easily caught, and since they have no means of protection such as the professional criminal has established are easily convicted.(54)

Recent textbooks do not include the habitual offender as an identifiable category, possibly because the term could be construed erroneously as a reference to an offender subject to a mandatory penalty of life imprisonment under the "habitual criminal acts" adopted by many states (such as the Baumes Law in New York and similar statutes applicable to offenders who have had three or four convictions on felony charges). More significantly, this nonspecific term has probably been abandoned because an ever-increasing understanding of human behavior has brought wide recognition that offenders formerly grouped under this label had little in common except the repetitive nature of their encounters with law enforcement personnel. Consequently, prostitution, drunkenness, and drug addiction are now being considered to be subtypes of "public order offense behavior" by Clinard and Quinney,(55) and as "petty and miscellaneous offenses" by Bloch and Geis.(56) Gibbons ignored prostitution as he examined "patterns of sexual deviation (male)"(57) and discussed as "patterns of 'vice,' suppliers and users," drug addiction, the opiate addict role career, alcoholism, and the "skidrow alcoholic role career."(58) Roebuck omitted any reference to prostitution in the criminal typology he established for male offenders, but analyzed as separate types "the drug addict" and "the drinker and assaulter."(59)

It seems probable that Cavan's habitual offenders "who stand midway between the occasional offender and the professional criminal" and "are usually thieves of some sort,"(60) now appear as "property offenders" in presentations by Bloch and Geis and by Gibbons. The former authors envision a vast behavioral gulf between professional crime and white-collar crime "bridged most basically by the shared fact that all offenders employ illegal methods to expropriate for themselves material wealth belonging to others."(61) Gibbons is more specific in defining his subtypes, with the result that he might classify Cavan's habitual thief as "a semi-professional property criminal," an "amateur shoplifter," or "a naive forger," dependent on the type of offense committed.(62) Roebuck's concept of the "mixed pattern, Jack-of-all trades offender" was designed as a category for criminals "whose arrest records do not evidence a specialization in crime."(63) Although the offenses committed by the men in his study were quite different, this concept may be useful as we examine the offenses of women previously convicted on drug-related charges.

In returning to Reckless's concept of the career criminal, it is important to note his effort to differentiate between "ordinary" and "professional" criminal careers. His use of the term "ordinary criminal career" appears to be unique, but the concept is similar to that described by Clinard and Quinney as "conventional property criminal behavior" and by Gibbons as a "semi-professional property criminal role career." Reckless emphasizes his belief that the ordinary criminal career is different from the career of the professional criminal in origin and modus operandi by explaining that offenders with ordinary criminal careers: usually come from lower-class families; begin their careers as delinquent children; have early contacts with the law; display only limited skill and dexterity in their criminal activities; and may use force and even weapons.(64) Clinard and Quinney are more specific in defining "conventional property criminal behavior" as the end product of adolescent delinquent gang activities in which the members learn social roles, techniques and rationalizations for their behavior, and develop conceptions of themselves as criminals.(65)

In effect, Gibbons subdivides the criminal career category described by Reckless into three subtypes: the professional thief, the professional "heavy criminal" (such as the armed robber or burglar), and the semiprofessional property criminal. The last two subtypes are approximately equivalent to Reckless's ordinary criminal career offender, and differ from each other primarily in the degree of criminal expertise demonstrated. We shall return to Gibbons's concept of the professional thief, but it would not be productive to pursue here his notions about offenders who engage in criminal activities not identified in the arrest records of the women included in this study.

As previously implied, Reckless differentiated ordinary and professional criminal careers primarily by attributing to the professional criminal: superior personal attributes and social class; "skill and artistry of criminal technique" in the planning and execution of crime; "social acceptance in and by 'the profession' "; a tendency to undertake more difficult criminal acts with higher stakes; and greater ability to avoid arrest and conviction.(66) He believed that "heavy crimes" could be considered professional "by virtue of their superior execution and the high status of their perpetrators in the criminal world," but contended that "the profession of theft is professional crime par excellence."(67)

Reckless's conception of professional theft is drawn from The Professional Thief, in which Sutherland defined its essential characteristics to include: a complex of techniques, abilities, and skills "directed to the planning and execution of crimes; the dispos of stolen goods, the fixing of cases in which arrests occur, and the control of other situations which may arise in the course of the occupation"; status with criminals and others based upon "technical skill, financial standing, connections, power, dress, manners and wide knowledge"; consensus growing out of "a complex of common and shared feelings, sentiments . . . overt acts. . . . a system of values and esprit de corps"; a pattern of differential association with professional thieves and with others; and organization as a system in which "internal unity and reciprocity may be found."(68) Sutherland's "professional thief" (whom he identified in his preface as Chic Conwell) listed eight categories of professional theft, including picking pockets, shoplifting, confidence games, and "passing of illegal checks, money orders and other papers."(69)

More recent authors tend to include in their classifications or typologies some approximation of Sutherland's professional thief, although the concept may be identified by varying terms and may be defined to include different legal offenses. Bloch and Geis use the term "professional criminals" to describe "such groups as confidence men, professional thieves, forgers, shoplifters and pickpockets" and, as previously explained, exclude from this category "property offenders," whom they consider to be nonprofessional persons who commit robbery, automobile theft, embezzlement, and arson.(70) Conversely, Gibbons lists the "professional thief" as one subtype in his category of "property offenders," and defines professional theft to include the offenses specified in Sutherland's work.(71)

Clinard and Quinney describe a general category of "career crime" and use content similar to Sutherland's presentation to identify "professional criminal behavior"(72) as a subtype differentiated from "conventional criminal behavior" and "organized criminal behavior." Akers devotes one chapter to "professional crime," which he characterizes as "non-violent theft" performed by professionals, and cites Maurer, Sutherland, and Bloch and Geis as his sources for including, as "major types of professional theft," confidence games, "theft involving manual or mechanical skills with little contact with the victim," pickpockets, shoplifters, forgers, and "smalltime grifters of all sorts."(73) Roebuck makes no comparable use of the concept of professional crime, but includes in his six identified types "the armed robber," "the numbers man," "the confidence man," and the "Jack-of-all trades offender."(74)

In her chapter "The Professional Criminal and Organized Crime," Elliott defined the professional as "any person who makes his living at lawless pursuits – whether he is a smalltime operator or a criminal gangster with farflung connections with other criminals in widely separated parts of the country."(75) Akers deplores the fact that the 1967 report of the President's Commission on Law Enforcement and Administration of Justice adopted a similar definition that "means that any habitual or career criminal, however petty and amateurish, would be called a professional . . . and would include such a variety of offenders that little can be said about professional crime to distinguish it from other types."(76) Akers, like Reckless, discusses organized crime in a separate chapter similar in content to the behavior system described by Quinney as "organized offense behavior,"(77) and by Clinard and Quinney as "organized criminal behavior."(78) Following their examples, the chapters that follow will consider professional criminal activity as a behavioral entity separate from that of organized crime. No further reference to organized crime will be made in view of the absence of evidence that the women included in this study were associated in any significant way with a hierarchical structure organized for purposes prohibited by law.

## SUMMARY

In this chapter an overview of relevant concepts, classifications, and typologies has been presented to provide a frame of reference for consideration of the data developed in this study. It may also serve to indicate, in some degree, both the absence and the presence of continued areas of agreement and the need for further research.

## NOTES

(1) Richard R. Korn and Lloyd W. McCorkle, Criminology and Penology (New York: Holt, 1959), p. 142.

(2) Walter Reckless, The Crime Problem, 3d ed. (New York: Appleton-Century-Crofts, 1962), p. 75.

(3) Marshall B. Clinard and Richard Quinney, Criminal Behavior Systems, A Typology (New York: Holt, Rinehart and Winston, 1973), pp. 3-4.

(4) Ibid., p. 4.

(5) Herbert A. Bloch and Gilbert Geis, Men, Crime and Society (New York: Random House, 1962), pp. 314-42.

(6) Julian B. Roebuck, Criminal Typology (Springfield, Ill.: Charles C. Thomas, 1967), pp. 97-104.

(7) Don C. Gibbons, Society, Crime and Criminal Careers, 2d ed. (Englewood Cliffs, N.J.: Prentice-Hall, 1973), pp. 300-23.

(8) S.H. Reimer, "Embezzlement: Pathological Basis," Journal of Criminal Law and Criminology 32 (1941): 411-23.

(9) Edwin M. Lemert, "An Isolation and Closure Theory of Naive Check Forgery," Journal of Criminal Law, Criminology and Police Science 44 (September-October 1953): 296-307.

(10) Edwin M. Lemert, "The Behavior of the Systematic Check Forger," Social Problems 6 (Fall 1958): 14-148.

(11) Edwin H. Sutherland and Donald R. Cressey, Principles of Criminology, 6th ed. (New York: Lippincott, 1960), p. 220.

(12) Ibid., p. 238.

(13) Donald R. Cressey, A Study in the Social Psychology of Embezzlement: Other People's Money (Glencoe, Ill.: Free Press, 1953), p. 20.

(14) Korn and McCorkle, Criminology and Penology, p. 145.

(15) Cesare Lombroso and William Ferrero, The Female Offender (New York: Appleton, 1900), p. 147.

(16) Ibid., p. 148.

(17) Ibid., p. 162.

(18) Ibid., p. 196.

(19) Ibid., p. 206.

(20) Ibid., pp. 219-313.

(21) Korn and McCorkle, Criminology and Penology, p. 222.

(22) Ellen Berscheid and Elaine Walster, "Beauty and the Beast," Psychology Today 5 (March 1972): 42-46. See also Karen K. Dion, "Physical Attractiveness and Evaluation of Children's Transgressions," Journal of Personality and Social Psychology 24 (1972): 207-13.

(23) Korn and McCorkle, Criminology and Penology, p. 23.

(24) Ibid., pp. 147-95, Ch. 9.

(25) Otto Pollak, The Criminality of Women (New York: A.S. Barnes, 1950), p. xix.

(26) Ibid., p. 88.

(27) Ibid., p. 161.

(28) Korn and McCorkle, Criminology and Penology, p. 146.

(29) Ibid., p. 148.

(30) Mabel A. Elliott, Crime in Modern Society (New York: Harper & Brothers, 1952), p. 201.

(31) Gibbons, Society, Crime and Criminal Careers, p. 219.

(32) Ibid., p. 347.

(33) Ruth Shonle Cavan, Criminology (New York: Crowell, 1948), pp. 182-203.

(34) Ibid., p. 182.

(35) Ibid., pp. 183-95.

(36) Henry E. Barnes and Negley K. Teeters, New Horizons in Criminology, 3d ed. (Englewood Cliffs, N.J.: Prentice-Hall, 1964), pp. 51-58.

(37) Clinard and Quinney, Criminal Behavior Systems, p. 192.

(38) Gibbons, Society, Crime and Criminal Careers, pp. 261-348.

(39) Manfred S. Guttmacher, "The Psychiatric Approach to Crime and Correction," in Criminal Psychology, ed. Richard W. Nice (New York: Philosophical Library, 1962), pp. 112-42.

(40) David Abrahamson, The Psychology of Crime (New York: Columbia University Press, 1960), pp. 124-44.

(41) Edwin H. Sutherland, "White Collar Criminality," American Sociological Review 5 (February 1940): 1-12.

(42) Edwin H. Sutherland, White Collar Crime (New York: Holt, Rinehart and Winston, 1949), p. 9.

(43) Edwin H. Sutherland, "The White Collar Criminal," in Encyclopedia of Criminology, ed. Vernon C. Branham and Samuel B. Kutash (New York: Philosophical Library, 1949), p. 511.
(44) Bloch and Geis, Men, Crime and Society, p. 402.
(45) Gibbons, Society, Crime and Criminal Careers, p. 326.
(46) Ibid.
(47) Ronald L. Akers, Deviant Behavior: A Social Learning Approach (Belmont, Calif.: Wadsworth, 1953), p. 179.
(48) Reckless, Crime Problem, pp. 159-60.
(49) Ibid., p. 160.
(50) Alfred R. Lindesmith and H. Warren Dunham, "Some Principles of Criminal Typology," Social Forces 19 (March 1941): 307-14.
(51) Reckless, Crime Problem, pp. 159-60.
(52) Cavan, Criminology, pp. 204-22.
(53) Ibid., p. 204.
(54) Ibid., p. 218.
(55) Clinard and Quinney, Criminal Behavior Systems, pp. 78-121.
(56) Bloch and Geis, Men, Crime and Society, pp. 344-75.
(57) Gibbons, Society, Crime and Criminal Careers, pp. 374-410.
(58) Ibid., pp. 412-41.
(59) Roebuck, Criminal Typology, pp. 118-35, 155-71.
(60) Cavan, Criminology, p. 218.
(61) Bloch and Geis, Men, Crime and Society, p. 320.
(62) Gibbons, Society, Crime and Criminal Careers, pp. 273-77, 300-11.
(63) Roebuck, Criminal Typology, p. 172.
(64) Reckless, Crime Problem, pp. 153-54.
(65) Clinard and Quinney, Criminal Behavior Systems, pp. 132-36.
(66) Reckless, Crime Problem, p. 165.
(67) Ibid., pp. 170-71.
(68) Edwin H. Sutherland, The Professional Thief (Chicago: University of Chicago Press, 1937), pp. 197-211.
(69) Ibid., p. 43.
(70) Bloch and Geis, Men, Crime and Society, pp. 191, 313-43.
(71) Gibbons, Society, Crime and Criminal Careers, pp. 261-73.
(72) Clinard and Quinney, Criminal Behavior Systems, pp. 246-61.
(73) Akers, Deviant Behavior, pp. 193-94.
(74) Roebuck, Criminal Typology, pp. 106-16, 136-51, 172-99.
(75) Elliott, Crime in Modern Society, p. 136.
(76) Akers, Deviant Behavior, p. 194.
(77) Richard Quinney, The Social Reality of Crime (Boston: Little, Brown, 1970), pp. 268-70.
(78) Clinard and Quinney, Criminal Behavior Systems, pp. 224-45.

# 3

# METHODOLOGY

This study was initially designed to replicate, in an institution for women, Cressey's study of the criminal violation of financial trust.(1) However, it was subsequently expanded to include an exploratory investigation of the characteristics of other women convicted of similar property offenses, such as fraud, forgery, and grand theft.

The study involved two separate samples. The analysis of data produced three general categories that may prove useful in constructing a typology of women incarcerated for violation of laws enacted to protect property rights.

In effect, the study proceeded in three separate phases of data collection and analysis. The methodology used in each phase will be described after a review of the assumptions that served as guides in the evolution of the study, and a brief explanation of the setting in which the study was made.

## BASIC ASSUMPTIONS

Investigators inevitably bring to any study a constellation of ideas, beliefs, and interests derived from their own life experience, the orientation provided by their professional education, and the purposes to be served by the research. The methodology used in this study and the conclusions reached will reflect, implicitly or explicitly, the following assumptions and beliefs:

- Women are people and may therefore be expected to exhibit a wide range of physical and intellectual capacities dependent upon their biological endowment and developmental experiences, and also upon the opportunity systems available to them.
- Each individual is the product of a genetic heritage and of the physical, emotional, and social environament in which that individual lives and struggles to find an identity and value system.
- Currently, at least, the behavior of women tends to reflect a socializing process in which role expectations are different from those established for men.

- Ethnic and class differences in value and opportunity systems, as well as physical and intellectual endowment, produce variations in the roles a girl-child will be conditioned to assume, and subsequently may affect the way in which she elects to solve the problems she encounters.
- "Offenders with similar offense behavior patterns are likely to share certain social and psychological attributes which differentiate them from offenders with other offense behavior."(2)
- Typologies are needed to identify, for further study, the kinds of persons who commit specified kinds of offenses under similar circumstances and who will seem to have certain characteristics in common – for example, sex, age, educational background, motivation, and attitudes toward self and others.
- For a variety of reasons, official crime reports probably continue to reflect inadequately the number of women who violate existing laws. This fact emphasizes the need to study the small samples of female offenders available under comparable conditions – for example, adjudicated offenders incarcerated in jails or state institutions.
- Efforts to identify types and subtypes of criminal behavior have value even when the size of the sample in a particular study precludes any claim to validity and can serve only as a possible stimulus for further exploration at another time or place.

## SETTING

The California Institution for Women is located approximately 35 miles from Los Angeles in a rural area equidistant from the cities of Ontario, Pomona, and Corona. It is the only correctional center for women operated by the State Department of Corrections, and usually has a population of about 900 residents.

At the time of this study, nearly 45 percent of the women incarcerated in CIW had been convicted of felonious offenses against property such as grand theft, forgery, embezzlement, misappropriation of public funds, and receiving stolen property. (In California, felonies carry a minimum penalty of imprisonment for one year in a state prison.) The 100 women included in the initial sample therefore represented approximately 25 percent of the population convicted of property offenses.

When the sample was selected, two types of records were maintained by the institution. A file card providing 13 items of identifying information was completed from data given by the offender when admitted to the prison. At a later point, a complete record or "jacket" was established to include, ultimately, the offender's official record of arrest(s), a social history compiled by the probation department of the committing county (including copies of any medical, psychological, or psychiatric reports obtained to support the required report to the court), and the reports subsequently compiled by the institution's staff (for example, post-admission reports prepared as medical, psychological, and educational achievement tests are completed and the resident's educational, vocational, and recreational interests are determined; and reports on the inmate's progress and adjustment completed by the psychiatric or counseling staff for use in reclassification or possible parole consideration).

## METHODOLOGY – PHASE ONE

This phase of the study was designed to meet the initial study objective, which was to determine, if possible, whether or not Cressey's conclusions about the conditions necessary to a criminal violation of financial trust are applicable to women offenders.

Efforts to select a sample entailed the same difficulties encountered by Cressey: "Persons whose behavior was not adequately described by the definition of embezzlement were found to have been imprisoned for that offense, and the persons whose behavior was adequately described by the definition were confined for some other offense."(3) An initial review of the cards in the institution's master file identified 100 women who had been convicted of related offenses and might or might not meet Cressey's primary criterion for violation of financial trust: acceptance of a position of trust in good faith.(4) To determine the answers to this question, their jackets were reviewed and pertinent data were noted. In many instances, however, available arrest data did not supply the information needed. Staff assistance was then sought to elicit a description of the inmate's offense based on information gained through daily contact with the offender. Through these procedures, 100 women were selected for interview.

The data obtained from these interviews and from the offenders' institutional records subsequently provided the basis for completion of the following procedures:

Two general categories were established. Women who appeared to meet Cressey's criteria were classified as "embezzlers" or "honest women who violated financial trust." All others in this sample were tentatively designated as "fraudulent operators" or "women who intended to steal or defraud."

Factor analysis was completed to identify the common characteristics of the women in each category, the results were tabulated, and case histories were selected to illustrate subtypes apparent in each general category.

## METHODOLOGY – PHASE TWO

The second phase of the study was undertaken in response to reports from correctional personnel that convictions on charges of credit card forgery and theft were bringing to CIW a very different type of property offender.

Discussions and exploratory review of relevant institutional records suggested the desirability of using, in this phase of the study, a process derived from Tyler's critical incident methodology.(5) In accordance with this decision, staff-suggested jackets were read until a repetitive constellation of offender characteristics became apparent. Inmates with these characteristics were not interviewed in this phase of the study. At a later point, women not previously convicted on drug-related charges were excluded from this sample. The findings summarized in Chapter 11 were based entirely on data tabulated from the offenders' official records.

## METHODOLOGY – PHASE THREE

In reviewing the records of staff-selected inmates convicted of offenses involving the theft or forgery of credit cards, money orders, or checks, some atypical patterns of criminal behavior were identified. Interviews with these offenders were completed and their case histories were added to the sample initially designated as "fraudulent operators." When the data compiled for the augmented group were analyzed, three subtypes were tentatively identified, their characteristics were tabulated separately, and illustrative case histories were selected for inclusion in Chapter 7.

## SUMMARY

This is not a statistical study, although some use is made of percentages in summarizing relative findings. No statistical significance can be attributed to the figures because the size of the sample in each category or subtype does not warrant such interpretation.

In general, orthodox methodology was used in Phase One to test the validity of Cressey's generalization. Subsequent phases of the study are entirely exploratory and can be considered to have value only if they serve to stimulate further research and validation.

The chapters that follow report the study findings and indicate a beginning effort to construct a typology for the criminal behavior of women who commit property offenses. This typology is obviously incomplete because it includes only the types of criminal behavior encountered in the evolution of this study.

NOTES

(1) Donald R. Cressey, A Study in the Social Psychology of Embezzlement: Other People's Money (Glencoe, Ill.: Free Press, 1953).

(2) Julian B. Roebuck, Criminal Typology (Springfield, Ill.: Charles C. Thomas, 1967), p. 16.

(3) Cressey, Other People's Money, p. 19.

(4) Ibid., p. 20.

(5) Ralph W. Tyler, Basic Principles of Curriculum and Instruction (Chicago: University of Chicago Press, 1950).

# II

# "HONEST" WOMEN WHO VIOLATED FINANCIAL TRUST

# 4

# SELECTED CASE STUDIES

The case studies in this chapter portray, in telescopic style, the lives of six women convicted on charges involving criminal violation of positions of trust they had accepted in good faith. These studies provide a basis for increased understanding of the offenses, characteristics, and behavior of "honest" women who appropriated money to which they had no legitimate claim.

The life histories of these women will be used as points of reference when the findings of this study are compared with Cressey's study of men convicted of similar offenses. Throughout the text, reference will also be made to the women described in this chapter as relevant typologies are discussed and appropriate classifications are developed.

## SHIRLEY

Shirley was the oldest of eight children. Her parents were divorced when she was 11. This was a heartbreaking experience for her because she loved them both and felt particularly close to her father. He had been a teacher on an Indian reservation and had seen to it that she was always exposed to books and intellectual stimulation. After the divorce there was a continuous struggle to determine which parent each child would live with in a specified period of time.

Shirley kept close contact with her father, but often the remoteness of his assignments made it difficult for her to see him and sometimes their letters were lost in transit. She did manage to go to business college after graduating as valedictorian of her high school class. She found interesting jobs in the business field but was restless and very lonely until her marriage. Her first husband, Paul, was a charming, handsome alcoholic who demanded good food, liquor, fine clothes, a town house, a weekend lodge, membership in a country club, and many other things she could not supply on her salary. Shirley finally decided to go into business for herself and became a licensed real estate broker. In the meantime she had one child, a daughter Diana, who was sickly, insecure, and full of fear that her mother would leave her. Diana grew to be very frightened of her father and indicated that this was caused by his sexual molestation.

Shirley was unable to keep up with the debt and continuing demands of her husband, who drank before breakfast and seldom functioned before midnight. Paul had begun to show interest in much younger women, and at one point Shirley learned that he was sharing an apartment with a young entertainer whom he had met in a bar. With the pressure of debt and her other unhappy experiences, Shirley decided she must divorce her husband because of his continued misuse of their credit. Paul was not particularly disturbed by her decision since he had other interests and had run into a lucky streak in gambling. In fact, he had made some rather lucrative connections in the casinos through his friendship with the young woman with whom he was living.

After 20 years of marriage, Shirley was again alone and with new problems. Her daughter, who had never been a well-adjusted child or adult, became diabetic and alcoholic. For many years Shirley had felt guilty that she had so little time for Diana because of her need to work for the things Paul had wanted. This situation remained unchanged because the debts Paul had created would take years to clear and she could not afford attachments and liens that would jeopardize her broker's license. At this point Diana met a man who had never worked and was looking for "someone to die with." During their courtship, Diana confounded her friends by saying that she was too sick to live and had been looking for someone of like need so they could "pull the trigger together." Diana, always a lonely and self-contained individual, had finally found Kee, a man who burned incense, sang to the muses, read The Prophet, and made his own sick interpretations of what he read. There was no formal wedding, only a brief service in a Reno wedding chapel. Kee kept his word and by morning he had pulled the trigger of his gun and was dead. Diana, appalled and frightened, ran to the telephone to call her mother, who had just arrived home from the Reno wedding. When they buried Kee, no one came to the funeral except Shirley, Diana, and Kee's homosexual partner. Three weeks later, Shirley was back in the same mortuary, choosing a casket for Diana, who had killed herself by overdosing with barbiturates.

Shirley now had no husband and no daughter. She was depressed, but less anxious about the debt because she had been the beneficiary of Diana's insurance. Then, as Shirley explained: "A few weeks later, a perfectly wonderful thing happened to me. I fell in love for the first time. Imagine, at age 55!"

During the years of her struggle with Paul and Diana, Shirley had developed a small coterie of friends that included a man who now became deeply involved in her life. She had known Corie for years in fact, she had once sold one of the properties he had listed and they had shared the broker's fee together over a martini. More recently, Corie's wife had been killed crossing the street as she was coming to meet him. He had seen her hit and watched her die almost instantly. He left town for a short time, then returned to the house he and his wife had shared for 30 years.

Corie now wanted to marry Shirley. He saw no reason for their maintaining two houses with two sets of memories of tragic deaths when they could be of help to each other. Shirley agreed but could not tell Corie about the remaining debts she had incurred to meet Paul's demands. She begged for time, but could give no reason except the truth, which she preferred not to share. Shirley then signed a usurious note, advancing $15,000 she had received from a client to secure the use of $75,000 for a period of 90 days. Now, feeling that the debts were pretty well covered, she married Corie and they departed for a brief honeymoon in the Grand Tetons. Shirley admitted that she had no idea where she would get the $75,000 she owed, but believed she could raise that much money on some piece of property she owned in another state. Her client waited five days for the completion of his purchase but Shirley was unable to meet her obligation. This led to her arrest. Since she had no prior arrests, Shirley was convicted of grant theft and sentenced to a prison term of six months to ten years.

At the termination of her fifth year in prison, Shirley divorced Corie because she was convinced that her prison term would reflect on his reputation as a reliable and honest businessman.

## SHIRLEY'S RATIONALIZATION

"My story would make a good TV pilot, wouldn't it? It has all been so unbelievable and I know I handled things all wrong. I should have known that Paul was an incurable ladies' man. He seemed to get younger while I got older; it was really weird! I should have been able to see Diana's problems in a more motherly way, and to recognize a 'queer' when I saw one. Kee was a poor little scrawny devil . . . and Diana wanted to mother him. I never knew about the suicide pact. . . . I still don't want to believe it. But I'm finally now, at 61, doing something decent. . . . I'm giving Corie his freedom. I've been a crook, a cheat. . . . I deliberately cheated a client and I deserve to be right here and Corie deserves to find someone who is right and good for him."

## GRETA

Greta was reared in an upper middle-class home. There were no marital or other serious problems in her family. She was the oldest of three children and the only girl. She had a good relationship with her brothers and they often shared with her their ideas about life, about themselves, and about the future. Greta graduated from a highly regarded university with a degree in business administration and wanted to be an investment broker. Her brothers chose other professions and fulfilled their ambitions.

Greta's parents had high marital aspirations for her. Her father was a successful physician in general practice. Her mother had not gone beyond high school. Her husband's irregular hours and the responsibilities of caring for three children did not provide an opportunity for further education. She regretted and resented this and sometimes avoided the Women's Medical Auxiliary functions because she felt undereducated and uncomfortable with her peers. The more she deprived herself of these contacts, the more insistent she became that Greta would have a successful business career and would meet an eligible bachelor in the process.

Greta turned to an old friend of the family for her first job. George Gregory had one of the fastest growing brokerage-investment firms in the state. He had liked Greta from the days when she played with his children, through the years in which she had been a babysitter for his first grandchild. He had, in fact, known Greta all of her life. Her father had delivered his four children.

Greta tackled her job enthusiastically. She began as a teller and did simple audits at first, under supervision. She also learned a great deal about the flow of money in and out of the organization. As she learned about investments she was given more and more responsibility and, at the end of her fifth year with Gregory Associates, was promoted to investment counselor. She loved her new job, was very good at it, and earned an excellent profit-sharing salary.

Greta met her husband exactly as her mother had envisioned she might. John, representing his own newly established one-man auditing firm, came to a regional meeting of investment brokers, hoping to meet potential clients and subsequently get contracts for his services. He was well dressed, and talked to the various brokers with quiet assurance, handing his business card to them in just the proper manner and making an excellent impression for his fledgling agency. Greta and John met on the first day of the conference and were married a few months later.

After their marriage, Greta discovered some worrisome things. John's income was almost nonexistent. His well-tailored clothes were not paid for and his apartment rent had not been paid for several months. He had leased the two impressive cars he was driving and was acting only as a caretaker for a rather luxurious houseboat while its owner was in Europe. When these facts became apparent, Greta's greatest concerns were to help John clear his debts and to keep her parents from finding out the truth about his financial condition. John had not been a high-living, fun-loving man who had no scruples about his debts. He had, however, been very poorly advised on how to make an impression on the clientele he sought to attract. John was not the country-club type; he hated golf, played it badly, and found few advantages in letting his clubmates know that he had none of their athletic drives or skills. Nevertheless, he had tried to look, act, and live like a successful man. John really had no need for any of these props as he had a great deal to offer without them.

Greta's employer knew nothing about John's network of debt when he called her into his office one afternoon. It was only the third time in six years that she had been so summoned. Each time it had been a happy occasion because she had been complimented for her work and given a promotion. This time, Mr. Gregory rose as she entered, as did three members of the board of directors. They smiled as he told her with pride that she had been promoted to be secretary-treasurer of the firm. Greta was overcome and deeply grateful. There were some misgivings in her mind, however, since she had assured John, at least tentatively, that she would quit Gregory Associates at the end of the year and become John's partner in the auditing firm. John's quiet soft sell was finally paying off and the number of his accounts was growing.

That night John and Greta planned how she could be secretary-treasurer of both firms without conflict of interest. This was the plan that unwittingly gave Greta her opportunity to become a master at embezzlement. There is no evidence that this development was in the mind of either. Opportunity proved to be the catalyst, not any premeditated larcenous intent.

When Greta told her employer about the possibility of her dual jobs, he saw no reason why she could not handle them both. Mr. Gregory recognized some of John's limitations – a lack of capital to attract new accounts and few fraternal or business contacts. Each new client had been the result of hard work and patience. John had long ago given up the notion that if one "acted big" he became so. Mr. Gregory, himself a self-made man, admired John's ambition and felt he could be of help to him now that the two firms would be brought in close contact through Greta's involvement in both.

John had never been associated with a big brokerage operation and had little idea of the large amounts of money entrusted to such organizations. Gregory Associates, although situated in an urban center, operated like a small-town business. People brought in thousands of dollars, sometimes leaving without a receipt for their funds. They were confident that their money would be handled with care because it always had been. Gregory Associates had clients who wanted a safe investment, not a fast profit. Within a few months, John rented office space in their building. After this, John's auditing business, reinforced by his connection with Gregory Associates, flourished beyond his highest expectations. As time went on, however, John and Greta found themselves unable to separate their business identities. As Greta was given more autonomy by Mr. Gregory, she and John reached the point at which they began to confuse the investors' money with their own. It was a temptation neither could resist, and so the embezzlement started. Greta had long had authority to prepare and sign checks for Gregory Associates. She had never misused this responsibility, but John now came up with a modus operandi that looked foolproof. Greta started, as do most amateur embezzlers, by preparing checks for her own use and matching them with corporate checks for the records. The corporate record was purely fictitious since Greta had appropriated the money on the check she had written to herself. Since John audited the books of Gregory Associates, Greta could steal without fear of detection. In the first year she appropriated about $100,000. With this, Greta bought gifts for her family, paid for the care of an invalid aunt, made a down payment on an expensive house, and bought new clothes. In the next year, embezzling was easier and seemed less risky.

John had developed a system whereby it appeared that he was offering Gregory Associates more precise and sophisticated internal control on the flow of money. In reality, he was giving Greta more protection in her embezzlement procedures. Checks had always been made out in duplicate; John now suggested that they be made out in triplicate, assuring more accountability in case of loss or misplacement of the deposit or withdrawal slips. The third control copy, however, was merely a ruse to hide Greta's increasing defalcation. The new approach to embezzlement was complicated because the theft could lie buried in John's auditing procedures. Greta would originate a check to an authorized vendor or client, using a fictitious invoice number. She would later destroy that check and in its place disburse a check to herself for the amount and date indicated on the two file copies of the original check. Sometimes she would use a fictitious name so that a different payee would show up on the duplicate and triplicate copies. John continued to give Gregory Associates a good audit although, at the end of the third year, Greta had stolen a grand total of more than $250,000. Their most pressing problem was what to do with all that money without arousing suspicion. Deposits were made in out-of-town banks, expensive home furnishings were purchased, and money was spent freely on entertainment and the acquisition of more real estate. After five years of embezzlement, John's auditing procedures were detected by a state banking authority and Greta was apprehended.

It was hard to convince George Gregory that Greta and John had become adept embezzlers. He found it difficult to forget the long years of friendship with Greta's family and the years of honest service Greta had given to his firm. For some time he and her parents hoped that there could be some way to save this couple from prison. When the admitted defalcation amounted to $350,000, there was little anyone could do except live through the trial and wait for the penalty to be announced. Greta was alleged to be guilty of 15 counts of grand theft, but her attorney was able to have these charges reduced to six, with a sentence of five to ten years. John received a somewhat lesser sentence and was incarcerated in an institution a few miles from his wife.

## GRETA'S RATIONALIZATION

"I never thought of taking any money at any time. After all, my employer was like another father to me; our families were very close friends. We never, my husband and I, planned to do anything illegal when we decided to merge, in a way, with Gregory Associates. It just looked like a break for my husband. He had worked hard to build up an auditing business and having an office at Gregory Associates was bound to help. Neither of us knows when we began to think of embezzling; it sort of happened and it did give us the kind of life and money we could never have had. But, I guess, what you really want to know is, did I have a guilty conscience when I was stealing so heavily? Did it bother me that my husband was my accomplice? I don't think that I thought all of that out. Once I started to embezzle, it became easier and easier to get any amount of money I really wanted at the time. In fact, stealing became like a disease . . . and I was hooked, like a dope fiend. I was weak and self-indulgent, but I hate myself for what I did to the people who cared about me and trusted me. My folks, Mr. Gregory, and the people I worked with. My god, how I let them all down!"

## TRACEY

Tracey, the oldest of eight children, had a very difficult and severely deprived childhood. Her father was a lovable alcoholic, who disappeared for several months each time his wife became pregnant. He would return home after the birth of each child, be an attentive provider for a time, and then leave again. Tracey could remember nothing happy or good about her younger years. Instead, she recalled the anguish she felt in seeing her mother suffer through these years of poverty, loneliness, and pain. She could only marvel at her mother's stamina and her willingness to welcome back and forgive a husband who brought her so much worry and gave his family so little upon which they could depend. Tracey remembered the quiet household, when the brood was finally asleep, and how she relished the peace of that quietness. The only sound in the big barnlike house was the quiet movement of the iron as it glided across the laundry her mother "did up" for some of the single men in the neighborhood.

Tracey managed to graduate from high school by doing housework for one of the teachers. A month later she was impregnated by her new boss, a married man twice her age. She quickly attributed the pregnancy to a younger man and, since he was unable to deny paternity, he married her. After the baby girl was born, the boy's parents had the marriage annulled and Tracey relinquished the child to a social agency for adoption.

Tracey was now 19 and a very beautiful young woman. After several years of many dates in many places and under a variety of circumstances, Tracey began to think about her baby again. Believing that another child might help to relieve the feelings of guilt she continued to experience, she married for a second time. Bob, her husband, was the kind of man she thought she had been looking for. A college graduate in engineering, he was also conversant with literature and music and had great sensitivity to the problems and needs of others. For some years he had held the same job as an engineer in a small valve and pipe-fitting plant. He did not have to exert himself mentally or physically and seemed quite content. What Tracey did not know until their marriage was that Bob was a solitary drinker, that he liked being an alcoholic and had no desire to change. She now had a 38-year-old husband who really did not need her. In a short time she realized, too, that Bob did not want children and would never give her the child she had hoped for.

For some time after she left her husband, Tracey grieved silently over her disappointing marriage and the loss of her "given away" child. To put her life back together she took a bookkeeping job with a local beverage distributor. Except for her boss, who was also the owner of the plant, she was in full charge of the office and of all fiscal transactions. Tracey was happy again and it seemed that she had worked through some of her anger toward Bob and was ready for a new marriage. She turned to Dewey, one of the drivers, a divorced man who had been awarded custody of his two children. Tracey was so excited about the prospect of marriage to a man with a ready-made family that she impulsively proposed to him. Dewey, a handsome and hardworking man, was flattered that this pretty young woman wanted to take responsibility for loving and caring for his children. When they were married, the children's foster parents were witnesses to the ceremony. Dewey encouraged Tracey to keep her job for a while since he had some bills and thought they needed some time together before they brought a six-year-old and a two-year-old into their marriage. It was not long before Tracey discovered that Dewey lived in a dilapidated trailer, had no savings, no medical or life insurance for his family, and no usable furniture. Although he had only a few outstanding debts, he was virtually penniless except for his paycheck.

Tracey was not daunted by her discoveries. She had a job that paid well and Dewey's driving job was fairly secure. They took a small apartment temporarily until the children could join them. Tracey was appalled to learn the amount of money required to support a family. Almost half her salary was needed for child care and medical costs. She had fewer clothes than when she worked as a domestic years ago. Dewey had one suit, two shirts, some tattered underwear, and two pairs of shoes – one for work and one for "good." Tracey began to realize that, although she and her husband were working every day, they were actually, by her recent living standards, paupers. The most agonizing part of it all was that things never seemed to get any better. One day the foster mother called to say that she could no longer keep the children, and so they came into Tracey's life for the first time. The advent of the children did not prove to be the rewarding experience Tracey had envisioned. There was not even a bed for the children to sleep in and their wardrobe, Tracey saw, was as threadbare as their father's.

Dewey found a house with two bedrooms and a large fenced yard, reasonably priced and clean. But it was an empty house, and for a few weeks existence was harsh and grossly uncomfortable. It was during those weeks that Tracey began embezzling, keeping up the defalcations until she had accumulated 179 instances of manipulation of funds.

At first, Tracey "borrowed" small amounts of money from the petty cash fund, never taking more than $10 or $20 a week that she very conscientiously replaced every payday. However, the empty rooms, the children's dismal appearance, their lack of proper dental and medical care, and the condition of Dewey's old car became a constant worry to Tracey. She had to have more money to have a better life for her family.

Tracey soon realized that the replaceable amounts she had been "borrowing" did little to meet the accumulating needs of her family. The chronic condition of not having enough income to "ever do more than exist" prompted her to withhold more and more money and to resort to a variety of manipulations. She postdated checks and receipts, stealing the money she collected. Because she had been authorized to sign checks, she made many of them out to "cash." Since she handled all incoming cash and checks, she did all of the banking and was able to use double deposit slips to shortchange her employer's account. No one seemed to question the deposit slip that she left for her employer's perusal. The amounts of money Tracey was stealing soon made replacement impossible; in fact, she had developed so many different ways of stealing that she forgot from which account or source she had appropriated funds.

During the first year of Tracey's foray into thievery, she stole $5,000. She explained to Dewey that her increase in income was due to a pay raise she had received. Actually, her salary had been slightly increased, so she felt less deceptive than she might have otherwise. The house was becoming nicely furnished, the children's needs were being met, and Tracey and Dewey now had some decent clothes. Her embezzling persisted, however, because there were so many more things she wanted for her family. She wanted a swimming pool, a new car, money for entertainment, and relief from the feeling of "having nothing."

In the second year, Tracey stole $6,000; in the third, $10,000 – still small enough amounts to be hidden by careful manipulation and by a new skill she had learned, that of keeping a double set of books. When Tracey was apprehended through an audit, she had embezzled about $27,000. She readily admitted her guilt, was convicted on four counts of grand theft, and received a prison sentence of six months to ten years. After Tracey had been in the correctional institution for about six months, Dewey filed for divorce on the basis of her criminal behavior and the bad influence this could have on his children.

## TRACEY'S RATIONALIZATION

"I freely admit that I knew I was doing wrong and would be caught. I had been getting violent headaches and nightmares during the last months of my embezzling. I stole to give my husband and my stepchildren the things I knew they needed and the things I wanted them to have. I had a very dear husband and the children were everything in the world to me. I guess I can understand why my husband is divorcing me, because I did disgrace him, my own family, and myself. But I wonder if he really knows that I did it all for him, and to finally have my children. Does he know what all of this means to me, how much I've given to them, and how much he has taken away from me?"

## TERRI

Terri, the youngest of six children, was deeply loved and overprotected by her parents and five brothers. Terri's father owned and operated a successful dairy farm that afforded the family a comfortable middle-class income. Her mother was a dedicated homemaker whose primary ambition was to be an adequate wife and mother.

In fulfilling the many obligations and responsibilities of rural farm living, Terri's parents were unaware of her loneliness. As a small child, she had no other little girls with whom to play. Although she became less isolated when she began school, this could not totally compensate for "something to do after school with other kids." Consequently, Terri began to read early and to excel academically. Her brothers were only mildly interested in school although they took part in athletics and never received failing grades. Having five brothers had some advantages, but Terri spent her childhood as a tagalong, seldom invited to join in the games and allowed only to sit by and watch the boys play. Thus she grew up in a world of men. Her mother was sympathetic, knowing that Terri lacked companionship with other girls, but she also found it comforting to know that Terri would be carefully supervised by her brothers.

Terri used her high I.Q. (135+) well. She competed in a national science contest during her junior year in high school and won a $5,000 scholarship. Her aptitude in mathematics and science, and her straight "A" high school average, assured her admission to any college. During her senior year, her father suffered a fatal accident. Although Terri's brothers had married and left home, they continued to work the family farm after their father's death. They insisted that Terri and her mother continue to live in the family home, but Terri could not accept the idea of staying in this remote spot. Her mother did continue to occupy the 12-room house, but Terri went on to enroll in an engineering school.

Terri loved the busy campus, the laboratory equipment, and the stimulating classes. However, she found herself again surrounded with men who, like her brothers, were courteous but did not include her in their informal seminars and colloquiums. She yearned to be asked to join them for a beer or a cup of coffee, but that happened only once during the first semester. Her male classmates openly admired her keen mind but continued to ignore her when class was over. As a result, Terri threw her energies into intellectual and professional pursuits. She tutored students in calculus and differential equations and enjoyed her role as a teacher. When the tutoring sessions ended, however, the fellows left. This pattern changed when one of her students, the wife of an instructor, became concerned about Terri's loneliness and lack of social life. In arranging a date for Terri, she selected a young businessman who was the favorite grandson of the town patriarch. The older man had carried on the family's banking business as his father and grandfather had done. He was the undisputed ruler of the clan, and it was necessary for any member of the family to get his approval before a marriage could occur. Luckily for young John, his grandfather immediately like Terri. He found her pretty, intriguing, and "different." He was curious about her interest in mathematics and science; it somehow put her a cut above the rest of the women in the family. It was this difference that he liked in Terri; he believed she would be good for John.

Terri was 21 years old the month she was married. In a brief period she discovered that she had married a man who was completely dominated by his grandfather. Terri's marriage lasted "seven ugly years" in which three children arrived, including a son, Hank, who was born without arms. John was aware of Terri's feelings of frustration about the kind of life they led, but this seemed less important to him than to gratify his grandfather's desire for more great-grandchildren. John reacted to his grandfather's demands by drinking heavily and suffering long periods of depression.

When the marriage was finally over, Terri took her children to her mother's home. She received very adequate child support until her husband was hospitalized for acute alcoholism and had no income. The patriarch, soured on John's "weakness" and divorce, refused to accept the fact that Terri or the children existed.

Terri now had to go to work. She could easily have taught mathematics or science courses in a high school or college, but she lacked a degree. She was almost 30 years old, brilliant, yet seemingly unemployable in any professional field. But Terri was back home, where many remembered her as a bright student who gave up a promising career only to have an unhappy marriage and a badly deformed child. When the county charter was amended to require the election of a full-time tax collector, Terri decided to run for the office. With the help and influence of her family, she won easily. The salary was adequate and Terri's intelligence, her sense of the logical, and her well-organized mind made her first four-year term of office a sound success. She had no difficulty in being reelected three more times, and had completed almost 16 years as county tax collector when she was arrested for embezzling.

During her tenure as a public official, Terri expended her energies on the two most significant things in her current life. The highest priority was her son, Hank, the child who had no arms. Terri's second major responsibility was to enlarge and modernize the tax collector's office. She managed these responsibilities quite well and was grateful that her two daughters were happily married and had developed into well-adjusted, normal adults. However, unexpectedly and quickly, Hank's hearing became impaired and his vision began to fail. He complained now of heavy pain in his lower abdomen, so intense that only heavy sedation brought relief. When he was 18, his legs were amputated. He then lived in a wheelchair, listened to the radio with the help of a hearing aid, and studied with a teacher who worked with home-bound students. He said very little and cried a great deal.

Terri continued to work, but Hank's medical bills were high. After her mother became ill she had to employ a practical nurse to care for him during the day. Her brothers insisted that Hank should be placed in a nursing home. They offered to help pay for his care but Terri would not hear of it, even though she was becoming more despondent, physically depleted, and financially impoverished.

Terri became even more desperate as she sat with Hank night after night. He was angry about his helplessness and the fact that he was being kept alive. Terri fought sleep each night as she tried to comfort him, but realized that she was becoming too exhausted to work and that a night nurse was essential. She knew only one way to get money to pay for two nurses and for expensive medicines. She began to embezzle. Terri did not steal with the thought of "borrowing" because she knew she could never replace the money taken. She only hoped she would not be apprehended as long as Hank lived. She never thought beyond that point.

Terri began to withhold money from delinquent tax collections because it was easier to delay accountability on these transactions. Despite her mathematical ability, she made no effort to develop a system to disguise her activities. She attempted no double-entry ledgers; she simply withheld money. Her sole objective was to meet her expenses without the help of her family. When the first yearly audit was completed by the state regulatory agency, it was revealed that Terri had misappropriated $20,000. Her brothers, shocked and embarrassed, made full restitution, retained counsel for her, and paid for a separate audit.

The court transcript revealed that the presiding judge was inclined to place Terri on probation because she had no prior arrest record and he found the reasons for her theft poignantly tragic. Nevertheless, he was forced to sentence her to prison on two counts of grand theft because she had stolen public monies.

## TERRI'S RATIONALIZATION

"I had great financial problems and I had a son who was useless to himself and completely helpless. My brothers insisted that Hank would be better off in a nursing home and they offered to help with the expenses. But I couldn't let Hank go; I just couldn't make myself do that. I'm glad now that I didn't, even though I'm in prison and I'll probably never be able to get a decent job again. They say people never forget it if you've once been in prison. But, as I said, I am glad I didn't let Hank go to be taken care of by strangers. He had so many, many heartaches, so little to be alive for, and he had to talk about it – just talk and talk. Who would have listened to him? When Hank died a few months after I was sent here, I felt such a huge relief, and perhaps a sense of foolish courage that I stayed with it all as long as I could. You know, don't you, that I didn't embezzle to get rich or to try to hang onto a husband or for some of the other reasons some women embezzle? I did it because I loved a poor, lonely quadraplegic that I brought into this world, my own son. Can the inverview be over now – and thanks for talking with me. Hank taught me how much it means to have someone to talk to and someone who really wants to listen."

## JUNE

June was 51 years old when she was arrested for an offense involving 15 counts of grand theft. She had no prior criminal record, yet in a little over four years of employment she stole almost $400,000 from her employer.

Her theft was from the A.J. Brownell Company, dealers in heavy equipment. June and Al Brownell grew up in the same neighborhood and went to school together. After June graduated from high school she did clerical work briefly for Al's father, founder of the Brownell Company. June left the company and married, only to have her marriage marred by almost instant tragedy. June's husband, Bill, became an invalid only a few months after they bought a small home on Bill's adequate salary as an accountant. He made a remarkable recovery, however, and although he could no longer walk, his arms were not affected and his mind was clear and razor sharp. His services as an accountant were still in demand and he earned a substantial income while operating from his wheelchair. June and Bill were now in business as partners, June making the contacts and attending to the advertising and other public relations work while learning about auditing procedures.

Their enterprise went well for some time until Bill's health deteriorated to the point where he was advised that costly surgery was needed if he was to survive. June then secured an accounting job with her old friend, Al Brownell. Because Brownell's work required frequent absences from the office, June was given a great deal of fiscal responsibility. To enable her to transact business in her employer's name during his absence, she was made the manager and secretary-treasurer of the firm and was authorized to sign checks drawn on corporate bank accounts requiring two signatures.

June soon saw the ease with which she could acquire money to pay for her husband's medical care. She began by writing a check in triplicate to an authorized vendor, using a fictitious invoice number, and later destroying the original copy. In each instance, June would then issue to herself a check for the amount indicated on office file copies. Her manipulations were temporarily foolproof. As a result, she embezzled nearly a half-million dollars in a four-year period.

It seems incredible that no questions were raised about June's new affluence and her extravagant use of money. Her husband had surgery by a renowned physician, and this was followed by a year of convalescence at an exclusive sanatorium and then by a world tour – first class. June was also generous to her friends and relatives. Yet no one seemed to question the apparent change in her financial status, least of all the man who had most reason to be skeptical, her good friend Al Brownell.

It is ironic that June's signature on a blank check eventually caused Brownell to call his auditor. When the auditor arrived, June made no attempt to flee or to lie. Instead, she explained how she had so easily embezzled over $400,000.

## JUNE'S RATIONALIZATION

"My troubles began with my husband's long illness and the high cost of his medical care. I am not 'a thief at heart' and I would not have embezzled except for the pressure of mounting unpaid bills. It was so easy to take the money. So many people had been good to us and I bought gifts to show our appreciation. I wanted my husband to have the best medical care possible because he had suffered so long. Then I indulged myself, too, in some ways. Right now it doesn't seem real; it just couldn't have happened. I hurt so many people, especially one man who trusted me with all the money he owned. Maybe when I get out of here I can make some of this up to those I hurt – I hope so."

## JAN

Jan had always been an incurable romantic. She grew up in a poor family. She heard endless arguments between her parents over lack of money, and often she and her younger brother and sister clung to each other and cringed when their parents' voices became louder and angrier. Sometimes, when the three children were huddled together in bed, they heard a thud in the darkness, followed by a low sobbing sound and then their father's anxious and tender voice. They knew he had hit their mother again and that he was sorry. They watched him come home from work too tired to move, too tired to be anything to anyone. They saw him lean forward in his chair so often, crying openly and without control, because he worked so hard and still the family had nothing. Jan learned how to escape the tortures of listening and watching as soon as she became old enough to read. She lost herself in books, mostly books about love and rich people. Jan's heroes and heroines were always handsome, beautiful, and successful. Her rich fantasy life made her less vulnerable to the poverty that surrounded her, and she never felt the isolation from others that her brother and sister seemed to experience.

Jan began very early to believe that people did not have to stay poor. It was stupid not to have decent clothes, to have to put your hand way into the collection plate in church so that people didn't see you put in only a nickel. It was stupid to have a refrigerator that didn't work and an ancient car that wouldn't start unless it got pushed by another car. She couldn't look at her father's lye-bitten hands and the fingernails that had grown thick and yellow, without feeling sorry for his stupidity.

Jan had grown into something of a teenage cynic. She loved her mother but grew to hate the monotony of the constant reminder that "money isn't everything; it's a family's good name that God adores." Jan drew no satisfaction from her mother's continual carping: "Yes, we are poor, Janie, but your father works at honest labor and we can all die in the night and know that our souls are safe with Him." Jan did not think it so gallant to be "pure but poor." This, she often told her mother, was "stupid."

Jan was not a pretty young girl, but she was witty, bright, and formed relationships with others easily and with poise. She went through high school with good grades and became very interested in art history. When she graduated, she had the choice of three scholarships. She chose a university that offered an excellent program in art history, which she supplemented with courses in interior decorating. But Jan was impatient, had some difficulty in living on a limited budget, and after two years left school. Jan soon found that she was equipped for little except part-time interior-decorating jobs that paid little since she only assisted. Because she still believed it was stupid to remain poor, she enrolled in night school to learn the fundamentals of bookkeeping. In a few months she obtained her first full-time job. Here she served as bookkeeper and office manager for two engineering-consulting firms owned by the same man. Her employer was a busy, highly efficient, and successful person who had little time for his offices and who did most of his work away from his desk. He was pleased to have Jan take on so many responsibilities and he liked her intelligent manner of relating to clients.

Jan worked contentedly for several years. Then, one morning she answered the telephone to hear her employer ask her to perform a different kind of chore than she had ever been asked to do before. She was to post bail for his nephew, who was in the drunk tank, having been arrested the night before for being intoxicated in a public place and for disturbing the peace. Jan posted the bail and was curious to meet the man she had just helped to liberate. She waited to find her "ward," a handsome man, looking somewhat chagrined and rumpled, but nonetheless devastatingly charming. He told Jan how grateful he was to her and to his uncle for his release and, over a cup of coffee, explained how he happened to get arrested. In his barhopping he had met a male transvestite who looked terribly funny in a sheer red voile dress and a purple-green wig. He began to "heckle the stupid old queen," at which the man threateningly approached him with fists held in fight position. Phil recalled gleefully that he told the fellow he "didn't hit little old ladies." Phil ended up on the floor and was hauled off to jail after the other man departed.

Jan was enraptured by this sophisticated, interesting man. She had never seen anyone like him. By the time they left each other an hour later, Jan was deeply in love. They had talked of many things in that hour and she was ready to marry, right then, a man who had never worked at anything for more than a week and who had been married three times before. Each of his marriages had produced two children, and he had not only been in and out of the drunk tank with some regularity, but had also spent considerable time in alimony row.

Within a month, Jan and Phil were married. He then became insistent that Jan show her love for him by keeping up his child-support payments so that he would not have to go to jail any more for nonsupport. He insisted, too, that she give him enough money to buy into a bookmaking operation that he believed to be "a gold mine." Phil liked the casino and bookie atmosphere, show girls, and the intrigue of gambling. Jan vacillated as to whether she should share with her employer her concerns about Phil, but decided that she must handle her problems alone. While it was true that Phil was her boss's nephew, there had been very little relationship between the two. In fact, the two men scarcely knew each other.

Phil threatened to leave Jan. Life without him was more than she could bring herself to think about; when she did, she would get sick and go into spasms of hysterical sobbing and acute depression. Phil was not impressed by these painful reactions, and only repeated that if she loved him enough she would show it by making more money available to him. He knew what her income was and that she was doing all she could to supply him with money, but he knew, too, that she worked with thousands of dollars. Although he never suggested that she embezzle, he exerted continuous pressure to produce more money.

Jan had never given any thought to misusing her employer's trust or his money. She had no idea how to steal, but she began by pilfering from the petty cash fund. At first she prepared checks for less than $100 because such small amounts could remain undetected for a long time. Jan was afraid to tell her husband that she had more money because she was afraid that he would demand still more. One night, when Phil was in a fit of rage because he felt she was "reneging" on her responsibility, she dropped $2,000 in his lap. Jan felt like a prostitute in reverse – she was actually paying Phil to live with her – but she lacked the courage needed to stop the thefts.

Jan was authorized to sign any check under $5,000. She now began to make out checks to herself in larger and larger amounts. Finally she issued, to fictitious clients, promissory notes amounting to $75,000. By this time, Jan began to lose her concern over detection: Phil was happy now, he had again become her lover, he had money to gamble, and his former wives were no longer placing pressure on him for child support. Acting on a tip from a client that Jan was embezzling, her employer ordered immediate surveillance and an audit. Jan was arrested as she attempted to issue her fourth promissory note for $25,000. Had she succeeded, she would have stolen about $175,000 in less than two years.

## JAN'S RATIONALIZATION

"I am here on five counts of grand theft. I stole a great deal of money in a short time and I did it because I thought it would save my marriage. I couldn't stand the idea of losing my husband, even though I knew he was a bum. All of my letters to him have come back, so I guess he's through with me. I'll always love him and I'll never, never give him a divorce, but I guess he can divorce me because I'm a felon now. I still think, when I get out of here in two years or so, we could make our marriage work. Yes, I know I did wrong, but it seemed to me that I was doing it for the best reason in the world – to keep somebody I loved."

# 5

# VIOLATION OF FINANCIAL TRUST

In Part I, several references were made to the methodological approach used by Cressey in his Study in the Social Psychology of Embezzlement: Other People's Money.(1) This chapter will: review Cressey's oft-quoted generalization summarizing the process he believed must precede a criminal violation of financial trust; examine, in some detail, the findings from which this generalization was derived; compare the data obtained by Cressey in his study of male offenders with those found in this study of women convicted of similar offenses; and end with a brief summary. Before any attempt is made to embark upon the stated objectives of this chapter, it may be well to reiterate some related content included in earlier chapters.

Although Cressey used the term "Study . . . of Embezzlement" in the title of his work, his initial chapter explained his decision to abandon the legal concept of embezzlement because his early case contacts indicated that it "did not describe a homogeneous class of criminal behavior."(2) In its place he established two criteria for use in selecting the cases to be included in his investigation and redefined the phenomenon to be investigated as "criminal violation of financial trust." As he pointed out, the basic requirement that "the person must have accepted a position of trust in good faith" is almost identical with the legal requirement that the "felonious intent" in embezzlement must be formulated after the time of taking possession.(3) His second requirement, that the person selected for study "must have violated that trust by committing a crime,"(4) enabled him to include in his study men who met this criterion even though they had been convicted of property offenses other than embezzlement (such as forgery).

All the women to be considered in this chapter fully met the two-pronged admission requirement established by Cressey. Without exception, they had committed crimes involving violation of a position of trust accepted in good faith. Despite this fact, only two women in this category had been convicted of embezzlement. The others had received in-determinate sentences of one or more years in prison after conviction on charges that included grand theft (most frequent – 60 percent), grand theft-forgery, forgery, misappropriation of public funds, appropriation of public monies for personal use, destruction of public records, keeping false accounts, and making false entries. In all instances, the nature of the offense appeared to warrant a charge of embezzlement. The fact that most of these women were not so charged would tend to validate Cressey's decision to identify factors common to this pattern of criminal behavior and to abandon any attempt to limit the study to persons convicted of embezzlement.

The primary goal of Cressey's study was

> to account for the differential in behavior indicated by the fact that some persons in positions of financial trust violate that trust, whereas other persons, or even the same person at a different time, in identical or very similar positions do not so violate it.(5)

His approach to this problem was an effort to determine "whether a definable sequence or conjuncture of events is always present when criminal trust violation is present, and never present when trust violation is absent," and to explain the presence or absence of these events.(6)

Cressey elected to use a method of study that he noted "has its roots in John Stuart Mill's 'method of difference,' was elaborated as the method of 'analytic induction' by Znaniecki, and was referred to as 'the principle of limited inquiry' by Lindesmith."(7) In brief, his methodology involved a trial-and-error process in which he formulated an hypothesis, tested its validity by record review and interview, made appropriate modifications in the hypothesis, and repeated these steps until he evolved a generalization that seemed applicable to all cases included in his sample.

In this study of female offenders, no attempt was made to continue this methodological process. Instead, the findings are merely reported and compared with the results of Cressey's study of male trust violators.

## CRESSEY'S GENERALIZATION

The final revision of Cressey's hypothesis assumed the following form:

> Trusted persons become trust violators when they conceive of themselves as having a financial problem which is non-shareable, are aware that this problem can be secretly resolved by violation of the position of financial trust, and are able to apply to their own conduct in the situation, verbalizations which enable them to adjust their conceptions

of themselves as trusted persons with their conceptions of themselves as users of the entrusted funds or property.(8)

Stated more succinctly, Cressey concluded that trust violation does not occur unless the trusted person: encounters a nonshareable financial problem; realizes that his position of trust offers a solution to his problem; and can formulate, in advance, a rationalization that will permit him to justify to himself a violation of trust.

In his final chapter, Cressey explained that this theory of criminal violation of trust produced no "negative cases" or reason for rejection when applied to 133 male trust violators in three prisons, or to approximately 200 cases collected by other investigators.(9) In 1973 Akers concluded that Cressey's hypothesis had stood the test of time because it had been widely cited for years and "to date no negative cases have been reported in the literature."(10) In view of these findings, it seems important to examine in some detail the ways in which the data produced by this study tend to support or negate Cressey's generalization, and to note any sex differentials that might seem apparent in the data produced by the two studies.

## THE NONSHAREABLE PROBLEM

The term embezzlement has long been associated with activities that men might be reluctant to discuss with their employers, wives, or neighbors. As Bloch and Geis pointed out, the word is derived from the French "bezzle," which means "drink to excess, gluttonage, revel, waste in riot and plunder."(11) As they also stated, some popular writers have insisted that embezzlement is a crime brought about by "bookies, babes, and booze."(12) Cressey alluded to the popular conception of an embezzler as a victim of "wine, women, and wagering,"(13) but insisted that such activities have significance in trust violation only when they result in a financial problem that the individual finds nonshareable, and thereby set in motion other steps in the "trust violation process."(14)

In discussing "the nature of the non-shareable problem," Cressey stressed the fact that a financial problem that one man might define as nonshareable would not be so considered by another.(15) He identified six prevalent types of problems, and presented excerpts from case histories illustrating the reasons that trust violators found these problems nonshareable. In our effort to identify any existing sex differences in situation and motivation, it seems useful to examine these categories as they relate to the data collected in this study of female trust violators.

## Violation of Ascribed Obligations

Under the heading of violation of ascribed obligations, Cressey discussed the behavior of trust violators who previously failed to meet "those obligations of a non-financial nature which are expected of parties in consequence of their incumbency in positions of financial trust."(16) He cited as examples men who violated written or unspoken rules against gambling or betting at the racetrack imposed by their employers and who, therefore, considered their resulting financial problems to be unshareable.

In the study of women at CIW, this type of problem did not appear in any pure form, though a contributory role might be ascribed in two cases.

### Doris

A 44-year-old accountant (I.Q. of 120) with four children and an intact marriage to a police officer, Doris became involved in a love affair with the janitor of the church where she served as a part-time secretary-treasurer. For reasons not entirely clear, Doris embezzled $3,300 from her employers (three physicians), borrowed money from her lover to replace these funds when he accused her of embezzlement, and was apprehended when he reported her theft to a law enforcement official after she refused to leave her husband of 25 years. Doris was unable to identify any nonshareable problems, but it seemed evident that she considered her extramarital affair a violation of the ascribed obligation of an accountant who had been trusted by her church and employers for 19 years.

### Shirley

Shirley considered her husband's debts a nonshareable problem that she must eliminate before entering into a second marriage. It seems possible that the nature of these debts may have seemed a violation of the obligations imposed by her broker's license (see case study).

## Problems Resulting from Personal Failure

Cressey included in the category of problems resulting from personal failure a variety of problems that the trust violator considered to be a consequence of his own bad judgment or stupidity, including one situation in which the financial problem became unshareable because his family had advised the trust violator not to marry a divorcée with five dependents.(17)

Shirley's nonshareable problem probably was not wholly related to the nature of the debts contracted by her first husband. In fact, her own words indicate clearly her belief that she "handled things all wrong" and "should have known that Paul was an incurable ladies' man." As a result, she was unable to share with her fiancé or business associates a problem that would indicate her lack of judgment.

Greta could not share with her parents the fact that her husband had moderate debts instead of the affluence he pretended in his effort to encourage the confidence of clients. It is probable that her inability to produce a "successful" husband may have aroused fear that she would be considered a personal failure by her mother.

## Problems Resulting from Business Reversals

The preponderance of women included in the present study were trust-violating employees. There was no evidence that legitimate business reverses had been experienced by any woman in business. It is interesting to note, however, that Cressey included in this category a bank president who embezzled funds in an effort to avoid revealing the bank's shaky financial structure, and explained that the banker's "previous success had engendered a pride in his ability to handle difficult situations"(18) that would have been damaged by his resignation or by the bank's failure. Although the circumstances are different, Shirley's pride in her skill at handling her business affairs may have played a significant role in her inability to share her financial problems with her fiancé.

## Problems Resulting from Physical Isolation

Cressey commented on the problem that is nonshareable "not because the trusted person is afraid or ashamed to share it, but because he does not have associates with whom he can share it."(19) Although the title he selected for this category refers to physical isolation from persons who might be of help in meeting a financial problem, one of the cases cited would seem to indicate a complete absence of any helping person in the current life of the trust violator, or an emotional isolation or estrangement from relatives and friends, regardless of their physical proximity.

There is no evidence that physical isolation, per se, played a primary role in creating a nonshareable problem for any of the CIW trust violators. However, emotional isolation appears to have been a significant contributing factor in several instances.

## Problems Related to Status-Gaining

Cressey described the individual with problems related to status-gaining as one who aspires to live at a certain level, and then considers this aspiration, which is essentially a financial one, to be nonshareable when it becomes apparent to him that he is "traveling with a fast crowd," "living beyond his means," or "spending his money foolishly."(20)

Conceivably, the title assigned to this category would permit the inclusion of problems that stem from a trust violator's desire to acquire greater status with persons in a primary relationship, including spouse, lover, or grandchildren. Despite this fact, Cressey's definition of the reasons a trust violator finds his financial aspirations to be nonshareable and the cases cited in illustration would indicate an absence of any intent to include this type of status-gaining motivation. Interpreted more broadly, this class of problem would seem to have marked importance in any analysis of the process through which women incarcerated at CIW became trust violators. Unlike Cressey's men, however, none of the 50 women seemed to have any need or desire to "keep up with the Joneses" in the office, or any ambition to attain or retain membership in a desired group of generalized others (such as a group of physicians).

In general, the women whose problems might appropriately be classified under this heading would fall into two groups. First would be women who pilfered petty cash from their employers ($3,300 to $4,200). In most instances, these first offenders probably would have received probation or a brief jail term had a prison sentence not been mandatory for the misappropriation of public funds – for example, extracting from the mail or cash register money received in payment of traffic fines. One interesting exception may be found in the case of Doris, the woman who "cheated" on her policeman husband and appropriated cash paid to her employers. Perhaps the court felt that the wife of a law enforcement officer "should have known better" or should be severely punished for her disloyalty to an "arm of the law."

The status-gaining aspirations of the women in this group appeared very limited in scope and cost – for example, the desire of a lonely 68-year-old municipal court clerk to buy gifts for grandchildren to entice them to visit her more frequently; or a vain hope that additional funds might sustain a first marriage contracted at 50 years of age.

In all instances, the aspirations of these women seemed to invoke a pattern of activity somewhat different from that of the men studied by Cressey. For the women, recognition that a nonshareable problem might be solved through trust violation appeared to precede any prior expenditure of funds in excess of legitimate income. In essence, they were not playing "catch up" because they had contracted debts or formed associations that could not be renounced without loss of prestige. Instead, their aspirations seemed to involve a future enhancement of one-to-one relationships that they believed or hoped could be achieved through money available to them only through violation of their trusted positions.

The second group that would come under the category of problems related to status-gaining would be women seduced by opportunity, greed, or success in meeting a prior financial problem through trust violation. This group of women had superior intelligence (I.Q. of 130 or more) and a high record of success in securing for their own use money belonging to their employers ($27,000 to $400,000). Like all trust violators included in this study, they were first offenders with no prior arrest. In some instances, their illegal activities had been initiated to meet a realistic and unavoidable financial problem, and had been continued only because it proved "so easy to take the money." These women will be discussed again with a group not clearly related to any of Cressey's classes of nonshareable problems, but are included in this category because they identified the second phase of their criminal behavior as status-gaining or self-indulging in motivation.

The following cases illustrate the manner in which women in this subgroup seemed to have been seduced by an opportunity to obtain large sums of money illegally. As a result, they became addicted to a continuing pattern of criminal behavior.

Greta was previously cited as a possible example of a woman who experienced a sense of personal failure because she feared her mother would be critical of her marriage to a man with debts and no financial security. From her statements, however, it seems more probable that her aspiration to attain quickly the standard of living maintained by her parents and childhood friends played a more significant role.

This would seem to be the most obvious case of theft initiated or continued for status-gaining purposes. Greta's marriage was followed by a considerable period of time in which her income and that of her husband would have been adequate to clear his debts without trust violation. As Greta reported, the subsequent embezzlement ($350,000) "just sort of happened, and it did give us the kind of life and money we could never have had. . . . In fact, stealing became like a disease . . . and I was hooked like a dope fiend" (see case study at end of this chapter).

June's husband required expensive surgery, but this was not a nonshareable or unshared problem. Although her motivation was mixed, it seems apparent that status-gaining aspirations played some part when she continued to embezzle funds to provide expensive convalescent care and a subsequent world tour for her husband, to buy gifts for relatives and friends who had been kind during his illness, and to indulge herself in various ways. Like Greta, June appeared to become addicted to the good life after she discovered the ease with which she could appropriate her employer's money (see case study).

Tracey's nonshareable problems were more complex and more tragic, but her continued criminality, like June's, eventually reflected a status-gaining motivation. After one year of illegal activity, the immediate needs of her family had been met, but Tracey had developed new aspirations: "a swimming pool, a new car, money for entertainment, and relief from the feeling of having nothing." Tracey, too, had become addicted to her success in meeting her initial problems and had then become involved in an effort to achieve her status-gaining aspirations (see case study).

## Problems Resulting from Employer-Employee Relations

Cressey described under the heading of employer-employee relations problems considered nonshareable by an employee who "resents his status within the organization in which he is trusted." He explained that this type of problem "may take the form of feeling underpaid or over-worked or unfairly treated in some other way involving finances."(21) The employee is unable to terminate his employment or to make suggestions that might alleviate "his felt maltreatment" in fear that this might jeopardize "his actual or desired status in the organization."(22)

None of the employee trust violators in this study seems to have had a problem of this type. Instead, their reasons for remorse frequently centered around their regret about the damage they had caused an employer who trusted them. For examples, see the case studies of June and Greta.

## Other Problems Resulting in Trust Violation

Cressey reiterated at several points his realization that: the six types he identified did not cover all situations that produced nonshareable problems; "the listed types of non-shareable problems are not discrete";(23) and one kind of problem may be present when the initial defalcation occurs and another as the trust violations continue. The validity of these ideas becomes apparent as we examine case studies presenting problems not covered, in whole or in significant part, by any of Cressey's categories.

Cressey insisted that, in all cases, the trust violator believed he had lost the approval of a group important to him because of some activity that occurred prior to the defalcation, or that he would lose such approval if this activity were revealed (for example, the trust violator who was ashamed to tell anyone about his financial problem).(24) As shall be seen, this statement does not seem applicable to any situations encountered by the trust violators in this study.

In a summary statement, Cressey explained: "The fact that a trusted person is playing conflicting roles becomes significant to trust violation when the financial duties or obligations necessary to one role are considered to be non-shareable with persons encountered while acting in the role of a 'trusted person.' "(25) From his case illustrations and prior statements, it can be assumed that Cressey intended this generalization to explain the situation in which a man is afraid to tell his employer, his clients, his fellow employees, or his own employees about financial obligations he incurred as a participant in an extramarital affair, as an unwise investor in the stock market, or as a member of a competing firm. For our purposes, however, it may be useful to examine this premise in relation to the interpersonal roles assumed by many women (such as wife, mother, daughter of dependent parents), and to attempt to determine whether they are in conflict with "the role of a trusted person" in the occupational world.

Because Cressey's study involved male offenders only, it might be expected that his classification would not be wholly applicable to the situations faced by trust violators who are women. As Elliott stated many years ago, "Men and women live in different worlds. . . . The driving motivations in the average woman's life . . . tend to be emotional."(26) At a much earlier date, Lombroso recognized that for many "occasional female offenders, the origin of . . . reluctant crime . . . is suggestion on the part of a lover, or sometimes of her father or brother."(27)

In this study, the trust violators' problems that could not be appropriately placed in any of Cressey's categories invariably involved some significant relationship with another person. Two types of problems emerged, differentiated primarily by the role played by the "significant other": problems that cause the reckless sacrifice of a trusted position, and problems involving pressure from a significant other.

## Problems Inducing the Reckless Sacrifice of a Trusted Position

In his description of the process through which his final generalization was evolved, Cressey explained that his second hypothesis was that "positions of trust are violated when the incumbent defines a need for extra funds . . . as an 'emergency' which cannot be met by legal means and that if such an emergency does not take place, trust violation will not occur."(28) This study confirms the wisdom of Cressey's decision that this hypothesis could not be used as a generalization applicable to all trust violators. There is considerable evidence, however, that for some women an appropriate modification of Cressey's abandoned hypothesis might explain both the nature of the problem inciting their trust violation and the consequent process through which the appropriation of other people's money occurs.

The women included in this group were essentially honest women who violated their own value systems. They more or less consciously sacrificed their positions of trust in an effort to meet what they perceived to be their responsibility as a wife or mother, or to preserve for themselves what they considered to be their most important possession – a husband's love. The behavior of these women, unlike that of the men described by Cressey, seemed to have a Joan of Arc quality. They showed a willingness to be burned at the stake, if necessary, to obtain for a loved one the medical care he needed, or to buy back, if possible, the love of a husband attracted to a younger woman.

When the financial problem was caused by a need for expensive surgery or nursing care, it sometimes seemed to be the solution rather than the problem that was unshareable or deliberately unshared. Perhaps in these cases the basic problem was that the trust violator was unable or unwilling to permit anyone else to assume the obligations she had been conditioned to believe were inherent in the role of mother or spouse. There is no indication that role conflict was a significant factor in determining the shareability of the problem or its solution, but the latter consideration is more appropriately discussed in relation to Cressey's concept of the rationalization required for trust violation.

For many women in this group, the emotional impact of the medical or marital problem they encountered seems to have taken its toll by blunting their judgment or preventing an effort to seek other solutions to their financial problems more consistent with their own objectives (for example, Terri's arrest occurred before she was able to fulfill wholly her perceived obligation to her quadraplegic son). Available information does not indicate clearly whether their disordered behavior resulted from intense concentration on their personal problems to the exclusion of more pragmatic considerations, or an unconscious need to be punished for their trust violation. Both possibilities would seem to have some bearing on the nature of the problem that caused such women to sacrifice their trusted positions and their own sense of integrity. The following summaries may serve to illustrate or clarify these conjectures.

Terri presents the most clear-cut illustration of the lioness fearlessly protecting her cub at all costs. Why she needed to sacrifice her own economic future, her reputation, and that of her daughters and brothers, is not wholly apparent. Perhaps the answer could be found in the early life she had led as an only daughter protected by five older brothers on parental command; as a student admired and ignored by her male engineering classmates; as a wife whose marriage failed after three children were born, forcing her in effect to return home; and, finally, as a public official whose salary proved inadequate to meet the ever-increasing cost of medical and nursing care for her dying son. Perhaps the fact that her son had been born without arms and subsequently became a blind and deaf quadraplegic made her feel that she must personally atone to him for his handicap and pain. Perhaps her physical exhaustion in acting as his night nurse after a long day in the office robbed her of an ability to think clearly. Perhaps a combination of these factors made it impossible for her to accept her brothers' offer of financial assistance to meet the cost of her son's care in a nursing home, or to ask their help in caring for him in her way – employment of two nurses after she and her mother became unable to provide 24-hour care (see case study).

June was previously cited as an example of trust violation to satisfy status-gaining aspirations. Some need associated with her perception of her role as wife apparently created a situation by which she was impelled to violate the trust of her employer when it became evident that her salary would not be sufficient to meet the cost of surgery and convalescent care. Her nonshareable problem, perhsp, was her fierce insistence that her husband have "the best medical care possible because he had suffered so long."

The point at which June's need to protect and promote the health of her husband was supplanted by self-indulgent and status-gaining aspirations is not entirely clear. Did she perceive her husband's first-class tour around the world to be a necessary part of his convalescence, a means of earning his eternal gratitude, or a way to impress her friends with her affluence and devotion to her husband? In any event, June's history of trust violation provides an excellent illustration of Cressey's finding that the initial defalcation may be related to one kind of problem and continued embezzlement to another. It will also serve to illustrate the way in which many women seem compelled to sacrifice their own sense of integrity to meet the need of someone they love (see case study).

Tracey, like June, was previously mentioned because she too succumbed to a temptation to "gild the lily" after her initial financial needs had been met. Like Terri's, her sacrifice of a position of trust was child-related. Like Terri, too, she seemed driven to solve existing financial problems by herself, refusing to share with her husband the fact that their combined salaries were not adequate to purchase the clothing required by his children or the furniture needed for their new home. In her panic over the discovery that her new husband was penniless, Tracey's behavior, like Terri's, assumed a desperate, obsessional quality as she became more determined to fulfill her dream despite violent headaches, nightmares, and the realization that she probably would be apprehended (see case study).

Helen, a 37-year-old accountant, probably exhibited the most bizarre behavior in her simultaneous effort to cope with the stress created by the long hospitalization of her daughter (nine months) after an automobile accident, and the impending departure of her second husband after he became enamored of a 19-year-old girl. Her appropriation of checks from accounts receivable began when her husband "was spending so much money" and continued for more than four years. During this period, she embezzled more than $192,000 from an employer who was forced into bankruptcy with no suspicion of her guilt, and $40,000 from a subsequent employer. In the last two years of her employment, she purchased jewelry at a cost of $48,000, including two rings for her husband costing $12,000 – which she subsequently sold to her employer.

Shirley should also be included in this group. Although other factors may have contributed to Shirley's sudden decision to "borrow" a client's money, some strong emotional need to go into her new marriage free of all past encumbrances seemed to drive her to a senseless act of desperation. Possible reasons for her inability to share her financial problem with her fiancé have been discussed, but do not explain her need to jeopardize her marrize and her future by attempting an apparently unnecessary violation of trust.

## Problems Involving Pressure or Persuasion by a Significant Person

Lombroso and his successors described the "gun molls" and less spectacular groups of women who have been led into criminal careers by a lover, husband, father, or female associate. In Lombroso's words, they are usually the women who "steal or compromise themselves for men's sakes without having sometimes any direct interest in the act."(29) In most instances, the women described by these authors acted as crime partners or as accessories in criminal acts planned and carried out in association with one or more male criminals.

Because we are considering here only the women who met Cressey's criteria, we automatically limit our concern to women who "accepted a position of trust in good faith"(30) but subsequently violated that trust in response to some form of pressure exerted by another person. Conceivably, such pressure could assume a variety of forms, such as seductive suggestion, instruction and example, coercive demand, or fear-inspiring threats. Conceivably, too, pressure could be exerted for different reasons, reflecting in part the relationship existing between the persons involved and the purpose it could serve for the "significant other" – for example, the persuasion or example of a fellow employee intent on buying protection for his or her own embezzlement; the cajolery of a lover who saw the woman's position of trust as a potential gold mine for him; or the demands or threats of a husband desperate for money to solve his own financial problems. In reality, this small sample did not offer any great variety of nonshareable problem situations that could appropriately be classified in this category. The following case summaries will confirm this point as well as Cressey's contention that no listing of nonshareable problems can be discrete.

Jan's employment did little to free her from the world of fantasy that had sustained her in childhood. Almost immediately after her marriage, her prince charming began to exert pressure on her to assume his child support payments, to provide the money he needed to buy into a bookmaking operation, and to finance his gambling activities. When he threatened to leave hear, she began a two-year span of embezzlement, which was the only means through which she could hope to retain her husband. Like Terri, Helen, and Shirley, Jan seemed driven to methods of trust violation that could result only in eventual arrest. In contrast to their self-generated activity, however, the impetus for her criminal behavior came from another person. Nevertheless, like Helen, her need to keep her husband became so acute that she recklessly sacrificed her position of trust (see case study).

Greta, previously discussed in relation to her status-gaining ambition, may also belong in this subgroup. There is no evidence that her husband placed any pressure on her to begin the embezzlement of funds, but his position as her employer's auditor created "the temptation neither could resist." Their situation and behavior tend to resemble the crime-partner relationship usually associated with fraudulent operatives. Greta is properly included in this sample, however, because more than seven years of honest employment preceded her inability to resist the availability of "easy money" (see case study).

Louise, aged 68, had been employed as a municipal court clerk for nearly 20 years when she was persuaded to follow her supervisor's example in pilfering cash receipts received by mail. Over a period of time, Louise had observed the criminal activities of Edith, her supervisor, but did not violate her own position of trust until Edith provided her with a rationalization she could accept. Edith taught Lousie how to destroy traffic citations and make false entries in the accounts to cover both their thefts.

Anonymous reference was previously made to Edith and Louise as examples of women who pilfered cash receipts in efforts to improve their status with persons they loved. For Louise, however, the desire to have additional funds to spend on her grandchildren appears to have been a subsidiary motive more acceptable to her than the precipitating process through which her own value system had been eroded by the seductive pressure applied by another trust violator.

## OPPORTUNITY FOR TRUST VIOLATION

Cressey devoted an entire chapter to an elaboration of the second premise in his generalization: violation of a position of trust occurs only when the trusted person is aware that a nonshareable problem "can be secretly resolved by violation of the position of financial trust."(31) In this process, he stressed the two following points. First:

> Trust violation . . . is possible only if in the experience of the trusted person, there is . . . specific knowledge (including

> technical information) that the occupied position can be used to produce the desired results.(32)

In this connection, Cressey explained that business associates sometimes contribute directly or indirectly to a trusted person's knowledge that a position of trust has possibilities for violation, and that observation of dishonest behavior on the part of associates may serve a similar purpose.(33) The experience of three women previously discussed tends to validate this premise.

Louise, the pilfering court clerk, was the only woman in the sample whose trust violation was encouraged and taught by an unrelated fellow employee. For her, the opportunity to pilfer cash receipts had existed for many years, but apparently was not seen as a means of purchasing gifts for her grandchildren until Edith provided her with an example and an acceptable rationalization.

Greta was taught a complicated method of embezzlement by her husband. Although she had prior knowledge of simple auditing procedures, the possibility of trust violation had never occurred to her during the years preceding her husband's appointment as auditor for her employer (see case study).

June apparently acquired her entire knowledge of auditing procedures from her husband. There is no evidence that he played any direct role in her realization that her position of trust as an accountant could be used to meet the financial problems resulting from his incapacitation and need for surgery, but questions could be raised about his complicity in the years of postsurgery affluence (see case study).

Cressey's second point was that:

> In some cases of trust violation . . . the technical skill necessary to trust violation is simply the technical skill necessary to holding the position in the first place.(34). . . It is also significant . . . that persons violating positions of trust do not depart from their ordinary occupational routines, the routines in which they are skilled, in order to perpetrate their crimes.(35)

Cressey's conclusions in this regard seem equally applicable to the trust violations of women included in this sample. Because most of these women had been employed as bookkeepers, accountants, or clerks responsible in some way for other people's money, it seems unnecessary to belabor this point.

## RATIONALIZATIONS OR VOCABULARIES OF ADJUSTMENT

For our purposes, Cressey's conceptualization of the third step essential to trust violation has great significance. It is here that differences in the cultural conditioning of men and women become most apparent.

It will be remembered that Cressey's generalization indicates a belief that trust violations will occur only when the trusted persons "are able to apply to their own conduct . . . verbalizations which enable them to adjust their conceptions of themselves as trusted persons with their conceptions of themselves as users of the entrusted funds."(36) In his chapter "The Violators' Vocabularies of Adjustment," Cressey made this concept more explicit when he explained that the potential trust violator "defines the relationship between the non-shareable problem and the illegal solution in language which enables him to look upon trust violation (a) as essentially non-criminal, (b) as justified or (c) as part of a general irresponsibility for which he is not completely accountable."(37) The findings in this study can be construed to fit within the general framework of these ideas, but many of Cressey's more specific observations were not reflected in the rationalizations employed by the trust violators incarcerated at CIW.

Cressey insisted that verbalizations that enable a trusted person "to adjust two rather conflicting sets of values and behavior patterns . . . necessarily are impressed upon the person by other persons who have had prior experience with situations involving positions of trust and trust violation."(38) He expanded this idea by claiming that the trusted person must have had contact with "group definitions of situations in which crime is 'appropriate' before such definitions can be internalized as rationalizations," and that rationalizations used "in the adjustment of personal conflicting values" must necessarily be "preceded by observation of rather general criminal ideologies."(39) There is no evidence that this concept is universally applicable to women. Instead, it seems apparent that it is wholly unrelated to the rationalizations used by the women who encountered problems that induced a reckless sacrifice of their trusted position either to meet what they perceived to be their responsibility as wives or mothers, or to preserve a husband's love. (See section on "The Nonshareable Problem" above.)

Women impelled to trust violation by some inner drive toward appropriate role fulfillment seemed to experience little conflict when faced with financial problems involving the health or potential loss of a loved person. When it became necessary for them to "adjust their conceptions of themselves as trusted persons with their conceptions of themselves as users of the entrusted funds," their behavior did not indicate any awareness of "group definitions of situations in which crime is 'appropriate' " or any prior "observation of rather general criminal ideologies."(40) Instead, they appeared to have been conditioned by childhood training, early education, adolescent fantasy, and adult group definitions of expected maternal or wifely behavior to feel that any conduct, including trust violation, is justified when it offers the only available solution to problems seriously affecting the welfare or potential loss of a child or husband. After their apprehension and conviction, most of these women expressed: great regret at any harm they had caused their employers and their own families; a conviction that they had no choice under the circumstances; a willingness to "pay the piper" for their criminal activity; and some expectation that others would understand why they felt it necessary to sacrifice their positions, their sense of integrity, and their future employability (see case studies of Terri, June, Tracey, Shirley, and Jan).

Some variations from this theme were evident in the small group of women who pilfered petty cash from public funds or from a group of employers with whom they had no personal contact. Unlike the women who felt their trust violation justified by the purpose for which the funds were misappropriated, these women utilized rationalizations similar to those identified by Cressey. The women who pilfered public funds seemed able to regard their illegal acts as "essentially noncriminal" because they were "not hurting anyone," while those who embezzled cash receipts from unknown employers tended to project blame onto other employees and to regard their own behavior "as part of a general irresponsibility for which [they were] not completely accountable." An example of this is Doris, the accountant previously identified as the wife of a police officer. She initially denied her theft, claiming that three dental assistants also had keys to the safe. Later Doris admitted her crime, but continued to insist that she had been entrapped by "the sloppy bookkeeping system."

Cressey established three categories based on "the system of trust violation"(41) used by the men in his study. For purposes of comparison, it seems desirable to list these categories (with necessary modification), though related content will show a wide disparity in the basic characteristics of the offenders included in the two studies.

### Independent Entrepreneurs (Cressey's "Independent Businessmen")

Cressey included in the category of independent businessmen:

> . persons who were in business for themselves and who converted "deposits" which were entrusted to them for a specific purpose . . . [after] convincing themselves either (a) that they were merely borrowing the money which they converted or (b) that the funds entrusted to them were really theirs [such as profits or commissions expended before a business negotiation had been completed].(42)

In discussions with former real estate dealers, automobile dealers, attorneys, and other independent businessmen included in his sample, Cressey noted a prevalent attitude "that everyone in business in some way or other converts or misapplies deposits so that it is not entirely wrong."(43) Even when this supplementary rationalization was not present, use of the concept of "borrowing" apparently enabled most of these men to feel that their behavior was acceptable or "not as wrong as 'stealing' or robbing."(44)

Sex differences in the two samples become apparent in examining this category. Most significantly, Shirley, the real estate broker previously mentioned, was found to be the only trust violator in this study who had been in business for herself. From this fact, it could be assumed that women who are independent entrepreneurs are: more trustworthy than men; more successful in avoiding arrest if they do appropriate client funds to solve their own nonshareable problems; or the courts are more lenient when a woman misappropriates funds and less likely to impose a prison sentence. Obviously, further study will be needed to permit any valid conclusions on these points.

It would be erroneous to assume that all female entrepreneurs who convert deposits entrusted to them use the rationalization through which Shirley justified her felonious use of a client's money. It is of interest, however, to note the absence of any well-formulated rationalization in Shirley's rather disorganized behavior and subsequent cerebration. Unlike most of the men Cressey assigned to this category,(45) Shirley made no reference to the concept of "borrowing," though she seemed to have had some vague notion that she might have obtained $75,000 from the sale of property in another state to replace her client's funds. The fact that she made no effort to liquidate her assets before or after her marriage raises question as to whether her sudden decision to pay off the debts of her first husband by illegal means reflected an inner need to be punished for her daughter's suicide, or at least to be denied the happiness her second marriage seemed to offer. Like Cressey's "borrowers" who were forced to abandon their rationalization in prison, Shirley looked upon her behavior as criminal and continued to castigate herself as a "crook" and a "cheat." She did not blame her behavior on "the unusual situation" cited by most of Cressey's businessmen as the cause of their difficulty. She projected, instead, the self-image described by Cressey's absconders, who felt that their crimes were due to a personal defect and that they had lost control of themselves rather than of the situation they encountered.(46)

## Long-Term Violators

With the single exception previously discussed (Shirley), all trust violators included in this study can be assigned to this category. Despite this finding, any attempt to compare the rationalizations used by these women with those of the men described by Cressey leads to an immediate awareness of significant differences.

Cressey began his discussion by stating: "Violators of this class usually . . . convert entrusted funds only after rationalizing that they are merely borrowing the money."(47) In contrast to this finding, only one woman in this category appears to have made any pretense of using the verbalization that she was merely borrowing the money she appropriated. This may explain, in part, the fact that many women in this group did not limit their peculations to "relatively small amounts of money."(48)

Cressey reports that other rationalizations appeared in a few cases, but usually assumed a role subsidiary to that of "borrowing." It is interesting to note that some men did rationalize "that they were embezzling only to keep their families from shame, disgrace or poverty."(49) However, it is important to note that these reasons seemed less acceptable to them than an illusion of temporary misappropriation of funds. Under other conditions, this finding might seem to indicate that male trust violators do not consider the protection of their families an acceptable reason for embezzlement. This conclusion does not seem warranted when it is remembered that all of the men in Cressey's sample had violated trust in efforts to solve problems they were ashamed of or afraid to share with anyone who could help them meet their need for additional money. Thus, it would appear that any misappropriation of funds to protect their families would also serve to conceal the fact that these men had squandered needed income through gambling or other behavior not approved by their wives, relatives, employers, or friends. Conversely, the trust violators at CIW did not create the problems they were attempting to solve through illegal means and were, therefore, able to justify their behavior without resorting to the self-deception involved in "borrowing."

Despite widespread differences in the verbalizations used, it may be useful to compare the behavior of Cressey's male "borrowers" with that of Tracey, the only woman who used this rationalization. Some similarities are apparent, but important differences can also be identified. Like other trust violators, Tracey did not formulate verbalizations designed to produce self-deception. Instead, she progressed through a minimum of three "vocabularies of adjustment," with considerable insight into her own motivation at each step. In the early months of her embezzlement, she repaid the small amounts ($10 to $20 per week) "borrowed" from her employer. (There is no indication that any of the men did this.) At some unidentified point, she realized that the amounts she could repay were not sufficient to meet the needs of her new family. As previously indicated, she then began a period of deliberate embezzlement in which her rationalization was similar to that of other women who felt impelled to sacrifice a position of trust to meet the needs of a child or husband. At the end of one year, the basic needs of her family – adequate clothing, needed medical and dental care, and dependable transportation – had been met. Like Cressey's men, she then found that trust violation had become "somewhat routine,"(50) but there is no evidence that she adopted their practice of "kidding themselves about repaying the money."(51) For another year she seemed able to justify the results of her criminal activities as well-deserved compensation for the hardships a cruel fate had dealt her, as a means of obtaining "relief from the feeling of having nothing." After she had indulged herself in a swimming pool, a new car, and expensive entertainment, this verbalization no longer served its purpose. At this point she began to have headaches and nightmares, and seemed relieved when finally apprehended. Like Cressey's "borrowers," she finally had been forced to recognize her inability to reconcile her conception of herself as a trusted person with her conception of herself as a user of entrusted funds.

Although Cressey mentioned the possibility of other verbalizations, his findings apparently led him to believe that trust violators could "remain in full contact with the values and ideals of former and present associates who condemn crime" only by using the rationalization that they are borrowing.(52) Because he found such universal use of this verbalization, he had no reason to relate the nature of the nonshareable problem to the rationalization that enabled the offender to violate his trusted position. In this study, it became evident that most women who became trust violators did not find it necessary to use the borrowing concept, but further analysis is needed to identify the factors contributing to this phenomenon as well as the verbalizations substituted for this rationalization.

As we have seen, women whose financial problems involved the health and welfare of a loved person were able to use quite comfortably the rationalization that they were fulfilling their obligations as a mother or wife, and to feel that they had not departed from "the values and ideals of former and present associates who condemn crime." The mental and emotional processes involved when women sacrifice their trusted positions in more self-serving efforts to retain or buy back the love of a husband are less clear, and very different processes may have been in operation when status-gaining aspirations assumed a primary or a significant contributory role in trust violation.

Cressey concluded that when trust violators realized their inability to repay the money borrowed, they "defined themselves as criminals, find this definition incompatible with their positions as trusted persons and usually condemn themselves for their past behavior."(53) He also explained that when they find that they have "slipped into a category [criminal] which they know is regarded as undesirable – they rebel against it,"(54) become "extremely nervous, tense, emotionally upset and unhappy, and to get rid of these symptoms they behave in rather incongruous fashion."(55) He believed this behavior reflected either a renewed effort "to maintain membership in a social order which condemns crime and considers honesty as an ideal,"(56) or "at least partial acceptance of the values of the new group [criminals] with whom they are now identified."(57)

It is interesting to note that none of the women who violated trust displayed any of the behavior that Cressey considered symptomatic of attempts to readopt "the attitudes of the group with which he identified before he violated his trust"(58) – for example, "report their behavior to the police or to their employer, quit taking funds or resolve to quit taking funds, speculate or gamble widely in order to regain the amounts taken, or 'leave the field' by absconding or committing suicide."(59) This would seem to indicate that the rationalizations used by these women were as effective as the "borrowing" concept in permitting retention of their self-images as honest and trusted persons, or that they had "become criminals without intending to do so." This dichotomy does not seem to provide a meaningful basis for differentiating the vocabularies of adjustment that enabled these women to violate the trust placed in them by their employers. In fact, those who felt most justified by the purpose served by their embezzlement (such as Terri) seemed fully aware of the criminal nature of their activities before they embarked upon a reckless sacrifice of their trusted positions. The only women who appeared to "become criminals without intending to do so" were those who had no serious financial problem (Greta) or had none after an initial need for funds had been met (June and Tracey), or had violated trust in response to the pressure or persuasion of a significant person (Jan, Louise, and perhaps Greta).

It seems apparent that all the women included in this category did use some rationalization by which they could feel justified in violating their own value systems as well as their positions of trust. It is equally evident that their vocabularies of adjustment were very different from the borrowing concept upon which Cressey's men relied, and that they involved, in all instances, some emotional relationship with another person and some concept of role fulfillment. Further study will be needed to identify more precisely the rationalizations that allowed "honest" women to embark upon violations of financial trust.

## Absconders

Cressey found that the members of the absconder category are usually "persons with few primary group contacts and persons of lower socio-economic status [such as] oil station attendants, salesmen, hotel clerks, truck drivers, bill collectors and the like."(60) Only one of his absconders had held "a higher status position of trust such as accountant, business executive or bookkeeper."(61) Because most of the women in this study had held such positions of trust, this factor may explain the absence of women who had absconded with funds entrusted to them.

Differences in the characteristics of the samples studied are also evident in Cressey's finding that

> individuals who violate positions of trust by absconding . . . conclude that their attempts to conduct their lives on an honest basis have been futile, that they don't care what happens to them, that they can't help themselves because the criminality "in" people comes out in circumstances such as those in which they find themselves.(62)

None of the women who had violated trusted positions showed this constellation of attitudes. Shirley was the only woman who felt her crime was due to any "personal defect" or that she had "lost control" of herself when she appropriated the funds entrusted to her.(63)

## CRESSEY'S CONCLUSIONS

In his final chapter, Cressey reiterated several conclusions that appear to have little relevance to the findings in this study. To substantiate the contention that "women are different" in some respects, it seems useful to examine some of these assumptions.

### Selection of the Crime

Differences in the samples are apparent in Cressey's report that

> most violators have had as many objective opportunities to steal, rob, or burglarize as they have had to violate a position of trust . . . [ but ] the accountants, bankers, business executives and independent businessmen all reported that the possibility of stealing or robbing to obtain the needed funds never occurred to them.(64)

Cressey concluded that use of the rationalizations previously described "not only makes the criminal violation of financial trust possible, but it precludes other kinds of criminal behavior."(65)

Even in these days, it seems doubtful that Cressey would believe that the women incarcerated at CIW for trust violation had equal opportunities to "steal, rob or burglarize." These crimes would have violated deeply imbedded cultural norms defining behavior appropriate for women of their occupational and socioeconomic status, and would have required skills they did not have.

More important questions arise in regard to Cressey's belief that "this type of crime is selected by trusted persons on the basis of the rationalizations that are available to them."(66) In this connection, he explained that persons in positions of trust "have accepted certain standards of behavior including an ideal of honesty." Trust violators, therefore, find it necessary "to use a verbalization which would permit the commission of a crime while the ideal of honesty was maintained."(67) For the women in this study, this finding seems valid but irrelevant. The rationalizations used by these women enabled them to violate trust while maintaining the ideal of honesty, but there is no evidence that other kinds of criminal behavior would have been precluded in the absence of an opportunity to obtain needed funds through performance of their usual occupational functions. In fact, it seems probable that the rationalizations used by the women impelled to secure funds to protect the health or prevent the loss of a loved person would have been equally compelling had any other kind of criminal activity seemed a more feasible method of acquiring needed funds. Conversely, for some women in the sample (such as Greta, June, and Tracey), perception of an opportunity to obtain required funds in addition to those actually needed appears to have seduced them into the development of rationalizations by which they could justify their criminal behavior.

In summary, it seems evident that: perception of an opportunity to appropriate money belonging to an employer or client played a dominant role in selection of the crime by the women who violated positions of trust; and differences from Cressey's findings in this regard can be attributed, in part, to differences in the nature of the problems to be solved, the emotional intensity and cultural conditioning experienced in relation to these problems, and the kinds of rationalizations available to the trust violators. (It will be remembered that Cressey's men were ashamed or afraid to share problems caused by their prior behavior, and that they relied primarily upon a rationalization that they were merely borrowing the funds they appropriated.)

## Personal and Social Characteristics of Violators

Cressey discussed at some length his belief that "the personal traits of trusted persons are significant to trust violation only to the extent that they affect . . . the process of structuring problems as non-shareable."(68) He insisted that

> they could not be considered as "causes" of trust violation, however, since the perception of the relationship between the non-shareable problem and the position of trust depends . . . upon having come into contact with cultural ideologies which sanction violation.(69)

As generalizations, Cressey's conclusions in this regard seem valid for trust-violating women as well as for men. It is evident, however, that the "cultural ideologies" to which Cressey referred were wholly related to contacts with criminal behavior patterns. Marked differences become apparent as there is no evidence that any of the trust violators in this study had any personal contact with "cultural ideologies which sanction violation" per se. Instead, their rationalizations appeared to have been derived from cultural ideologies that present as supreme values the expectation that a mother will make any necessary sacrifice when the welfare of a child is at stake, that a wife will protect and promote the welfare of her spouse at all times, and that the acquisition and retention of a husband's love is of primary importance to all women's well-being. As a result, the "ideal of honesty" associated with the occupational role assumed in a position of trust remained unchanged, but was wholly unrelated to the behavior invoked by a need to fulfill the role of wife and mother in accordance with lifelong cultural conditioning. As previously indicated, these women were able to maintain the ideal of honesty, but were propelled toward trust violation by situations not of their own making. Like the women described by Elliott, they responded with behavior based on rationalizations rooted in the culture of their private world.(70)

## The Differential Association Hypothesis

In his effort to link Sutherland's differential association theory to his findings in the study of trust violators, Cressey expressed doubt that empirical tests could be made of Sutherland's basic hypothesis: "A person becomes delinquent because of an excess of definitions favorable to violation of law over definitions unfavorable to violations of law."(71) He continued to believe, however, that learned rationalizations are necessary to the criminal violation of financial trust, and that "contact with criminal behavior patterns" is to that extent necessary to the crime.(72)

Cressey's findings also led him to conclude that "a gradual modification of . . . values in regard to deceit, trust and honesty" occurs and eventuates in the criminal violation of financial trust.(73) Most of the examples cited are not pertinent to the types of trust violation identified in this study. Nevertheless, it is relevant to note that some long-term violators (such as Greta, June, and Tracey) seemed to experience a gradual erosion of values similar to Cressey's finding that "the violation of trust was the culmination of a long process of modification of values concerning the inviolability of trust."(74) Other similarities were not present, however. None of the trust violators in this study experienced "a series of incidents or a critical incident which psychologically and physically isolated the person from groups containing ideal-type honest members" in such a way as to produce "an excess of contacts with criminal behavior patterns."(75) As previously indicated, a few women may have felt some guilt about having violated their own perception of the ascribed obligations of an accountant (Doris) or a licensed real estate broker (Shirley), or experienced a sense of personal failure with respect to some segment of their private lives (Shirley and Greta). Their situations, however, did not include "the presence of a condition which makes it necessary to deceive the trustor or makes it relatively easy for the trusted person to deceive him further by trust violation."(76) In all these cases, in fact, the persons to be deceived were not those harmed by trust violation, and the rationalization used had no relation to the person(s) whose trust was violated.

In general, the only women who seemed to have an "excess of contacts with criminal behavior patterns"(77) were those who experienced pressure or persuasion by a significant person (Jan, Greta, Louise, and probably Helen). As in Cressey's study, a few employees (such as Louise) observed an associate pilfering their employer's funds. Several others were pressured by their husbands to provide funds in excess of their salaries (Jan and Helen), and therefore may have been exposed directly or indirectly to an excess of contacts with criminal behavior patterns. In one instance, a couple (Greta and her husband) seemed to have been so seduced by opportunity and greed that they developed their own criminal behavior patterns through misuse of their occupational skills.

As we have seen, most of the women who violated trust were impelled to do so for reasons associated with their perceptions of their roles as mothers or wives. Thus, we may conclude that an excess of contacts with criminal behavior patterns may tend to erode the value systems of "honest" women, but this is not essential to their violation of trust.

## SUMMARY

This chapter reviewed the premises on which Cressey based his conclusion that a defined process must precede any criminal violation of financial trust. The data also identify apparent similarities and differences in: the problems motivating men and women who violate positions of trust; their opportunities for trust violation; and the rationalizations by which they justify their appropriation of other people's money. Most importantly, this chapter provides a basis for the conclusions and typology in the following chapter.

NOTES

(1) Donald R. Cressey, A Study in the Social Psychology of Embezzlement: Other People's Money (Glencoe, Ill.: Free Press, 1953), title page.
(2) Ibid., p. 19.
(3) Ibid., p. 20.
(4) Ibid.
(5) Ibid., p. 21.
(6) Ibid.
(7) Ibid., p. 14.
(8) Ibid., p. 30.
(9) Ibid., p. 156.
(10) Ronald L. Akers, Deviant Behavior (Belmont, Calif.: Wadsworth, 1973), p. 190.
(11) Herbert A. Bloch and Gilbert Geis, Man, Crime and Society (New York: Random House, 1962), p. 336.
(12) Ibid.
(13) Cressey, Other People's Money, p. 154.
(14) Ibid., p. 146.
(15) Ibid., p. 34.
(16) Ibid., p. 36.
(17) Ibid., pp. 42-44.
(18) Ibid., p. 46.
(19) Ibid., p. 52.
(20) Ibid., pp. 53-54.
(21) Ibid., p. 57.
(22) Ibid.
(23) Ibid., p. 66.
(24) Ibid.
(25) Ibid., p. 75.
(26) Mabel A. Elliott, Crime in Modern Society (New York: Harper & Brothers, 1952), p. 201.
(27) Cesare Lombroso and William Ferrero, The Female Offender (New York: Appleton, 1900), p. 162.
(28) Cressey, Other People's Money, pp. 27-28.
(29) Lombroso and Ferrero, Female Offender, p. 196.
(30) Cressey, Other People's Money, p. 20.
(31) Ibid., p. 30.
(32) Ibid., p. 78.
(33) Ibid., pp. 80-81.
(34) Ibid., pp. 81-82.
(35) Ibid., p. 84.
(36) Ibid., p. 30.
(37) Ibid., p. 93.
(38) Ibid., p. 96.
(39) Ibid., pp. 96-97.
(40) Ibid., pp. 30, 96-97.

(41) Ibid., p. 101.
(42) Ibid., pp. 101-2.
(43) Ibid., p. 102.
(44) Ibid.
(45) Ibid., p. 111.
(46) Ibid., p. 136.
(47) Ibid., p. 114.
(48) Ibid., p. 119.
(49) Ibid., p. 114.
(50) Ibid., p. 120.
(51) Ibid., p. 119.
(52) Ibid.
(53) Ibid., p. 120.
(54) Ibid., p. 121.
(55) Ibid.
(56) Ibid., p. 122.
(57) Ibid.
(58) Ibid.
(59) Ibid., p. 121.
(60) Ibid., p. 128.
(61) Ibid.
(62) Ibid.
(63) Ibid., p. 136.
(64) Ibid., p. 140.
(65) Ibid.
(66) Ibid., p. 142.
(67) Ibid.
(68) Ibid., pp. 142-43.
(69) Ibid., p. 143.
(70) Elliott, Crime in Modern Society, p. 231.
(71) Cressey, Other People's Money, p. 147.
(72) Ibid., p. 148.
(73) Ibid.
(74) Ibid.
(75) Ibid.
(76) Ibid., p. 149.
(77) Ibid.

# 6

# CONCLUSIONS

To conclude the discussion of the characteristics and behavior of "honest" women who violated trust, this chapter will: identify, in summary form, the areas in which Cressey's generalization is not wholly applicable to the women at CIW who met his criteria for criminal violation of financial trust; present a composite profile of the total sample of "honest" women in this study; describe the typology developed on the basis of these data; comment on the relevance of other concepts and typologies; and end with a brief summary.

## CRESSEY'S GENERALIZATION: AREAS OF DIFFERENCE

Cressey ended his study by reaffirming his finding that no man became a trust violator "except through the conjuncture of events" described in his generalization. He also noted that any research that produces negative cases will require revision of the theory toward a more efficient formulation.(1)

The findings in this study tend to support Cressey's contention that an "entire process must be present"(2) before trust violation can occur. In Cressey's words, however, "redefinition of the behavior included in the scope of the present hypothesis"(3) appears necessary before his generalization can be considered applicable to women who violate positions of trust. This redefinition would need to involve the areas of perception of the problem and vocabularies of adjustment.

### Perception of the Problem

Most of the women who violated positions of trust did not face the type of financial problem Cressey described as nonshareable – that is, one perceived to be nonshareable because "the trusted person is afraid or ashamed to share it,"(4) and believes that "his activity prior to the defalcation" has caused him to lose the approval of groups important to him, or that current approval would be lost if such activity were known.(5) Instead, the problems of these women usually stemmed from situations in which additional funds were needed to permit them to fulfill the roles they had been conditioned to perceive as their primary reason for being – their roles as wives, mothers, grandmothers, or daughters who must fulfill parental expectations.

In some instances, the situations confronting the women at CIW did not present problems they considered to be nonshareable (for example, a husband's need for surgery or a child's need for 24-hour nursing care). In fact, these problems were usually well known to relatives, associates, and employers. To cover trust violation motivated by problems of this type, Cressey's generalization would need to be revised to: include the situation in which a woman in a trusted position is unable to share responsibility for solving a financial problem that involves the welfare of a loved person; and to identify more precisely the "conjunction of events" that impels such women to sacrifice their positions of trust in an effort to solve their financial problems without assistance.

Cressey's hypothesis would also need to be expanded to include the situation in which a woman is induced or impelled to violate trust in an obsessive effort to retain or regain the affections of some significant person (usually a husband). These situations may be similar to the nonshareable problems encountered by some of Cressey's men. The essential difference would appear to lie in: the absence of any "activity prior to the defalcation"(6) that would cause these women to lose the approval of groups important to them; and in the trust violator's perception of her role and the obligations it imposes. In most instances, the need for funds in excess of legitimate income was created by the trust violator's selection of a husband. This act was not perceived as an unshareable problem because marriage to a loved person was an ideal sanctioned by the cultural ideology in which they had been reared, and preservation of the ideal was seen as a goal to be attained at any cost.

More study will be needed to determine whether Cressey's concept of the type of problem essential to trust violation will require further modification to accommodate the situaiton in which a woman has no identifiable problem, but is seduced into trust violation by opportunity when aided and abetted by a loved person (for example, Greta).

## Effective Rationalization or Vocabularies of Adjustment

Like Cressey's men, the women who violated trust were able to define the relationship between their financial problem and its illegal solution in language that enabled them to "adjust their conception of themselves as trusted persons with their conceptions of themselves as users of the entrusted funds."(7) To be applicable to women, however, arguments in support of this segment of Cressey's generalization will need to be revised to indicate that: the concept of "borrowing" is not the only means through which independent entrepreneurs and long-term violators can justify their criminal behavior; and the verbalizations used are not necessarily derived from "group definitions of situations in which crime is appropriate"(8) or "preceded by observation of rather general criminal ideologies."(9) In this process, cultural ideologies affecting the development of their role models (such as wife, mother, and daughter) will need to be recognized as possible sources for the vocabularies of adjustment used by women.

In conclusion, it seems evident that further research is needed to determine whether the findings of this study are valid for all women who violate positions of trust, or whether the results are skewed by the fact that many women are not sentenced to a state prison after trust violation (for example, women with small children, or women able to plea bargain when employers are reimbursed by relatives or a bonding company). Until such studies have been completed, it is not possible to assess accurately the effect of sex differences on the process essential to trust violation. Nevertheless, it seems apparent that negative cases can be identified in the case studies set forth in Chapter 4, and that some revision of Cressey's generalization is needed before it can be considered wholly applicable to "honest" women who violate positions of trust.

## COMPOSITE PROFILE: WOMEN WHO VIOLATED FINANCIAL TRUST

To emphasize the theory developed from his study, Cressey purposely avoided any comprehensive inventory of the personal and social characteristics of the trust violators included in his sample. He did point out, however: " 'Social factors' such as average age and social status are higher among trust violators than among other types of criminals because of the nature of the requirements for obtaining positions of trust, not because such traits, as such, have significance for trust violation."(10) He also explained that the structuring of problems as nonshareable, the verbalizations used, and other steps in the process essential to trust violation might be affected by socioeconomic status.(11) These findings seem equally applicable to women who violate positions of trust, but it may be of interest to examine in greater detail some of the other characteristics of women included in this study. As a preliminary step, it is important to remember that these data pertain to a special group of women serving prison sentences for felonies involving trust violation, and may not be representative of women who were convicted of similar crimes but were placed on probation or sentenced to jail terms.

In brief, the women incarcerated at CIW for crimes involving trust violation usually had the following personal, social, or behavioral characteristics.

### Normal or Superior Intelligence

About 50 percent of these violators were found to have an I.Q. of 130 or more. This group included most of the women who seemed impelled to sacrifice a trusted position to meet the needs of a child or husband, or were seduced by opportunity, greed, or success in meeting a prior financial problem through trust violation.

### Attractive and Trustworthy Appearance

Women without this characteristic probably would not be entrusted with other people's money, but age did not appear to be a factor. (Age range: 28 to 68 years.)

### Education beyond High School Graduation

All women had completed high school, one had a B.A. degree in business administration, and most of the others had completed one or more years of college or business college.

### Occupational Competence as Bookkeeper or Accountant

A high percentage of the women had these skills, but the sample also included one investment counselor, one real estate broker, one tax collector, and two court clerks.

### Stable Employment Record

Most of these women had held the same position of trust for a minimum of four years prior to arrest. (Range: 4 to 16 years.)

### Intact Marriage

All of these women had been married and the majority had intact marriages when apprehended. Most women had children or stepchildren who were adults at the time of their conviction.

## Responsible Status in Parental Family Constellation

With one exception, these women grew up in intact families. About 50 percent were firstborn children and about the same proportion came from large families (a minimum of six children; two had seven younger siblings). The latter facts could indicate a lifelong tendency to assume responsibility for the solution of their own problems.

## No Prior Arrest Record

None of these women had any record of prior convictions, but the duration of theft prior to their apprehension usually ranged from one to five years.

## Racial Composition

All women in the study were Caucasians.

## A Need to Solve Financial Problems without Assistance

Most of the women who violated trust began their appropriation of other people's money in an effort to meet an unanticipated financial crisis. For some (such as Tracey and Jan), no legal means for meeting a problem seemed to exist. Others (Shirley, Terri, and June) seemed impelled to assume personal responsibility for the provision of needed funds without regard to the possibility of seeking help from others.

## Current Conviction Based on Charges of Grand Theft

A few women faced other charges (for example, misappropriation of public funds, embezzlement, and forgery), but most convictions included at least one charge of grand theft. The sums involved ranged from $3,300 to $400,000. (Four women misappropriated amounts in excess of $150,000 each.) A small group of women pilfered petty cash, but most violated their trusted position by writing fictitious checks on bank accounts for which they had an assigned responsibility, or by withholding funds received for deposit in these accounts. In some instances, the preparation of fictitious checks required the forgery of a second signature, but the trust violators were usually authorized to sign the checks they used to secure illegal possession of their employer's money.

## TENTATIVE TYPOLOGY: "HONEST" WOMEN WHO VIOLATED FINANCIAL TRUST

"Honest" women who violated financial trust were the women who met Cressey's criteria for inclusion in his study: they had committed a crime after accepting a position of trust with no intent to steal or defraud. The results of this study seemed to identify four different systems of behavior for these women.

### The Obsessive Protectors

The women in the Obsessive Protector subgroup appeared to violate their own value systems and to consciously sacrifice their positions of trust in an effort to meet responsibilities associated with the role of wife and mother. Their behavior seemed to have a Joan of Arc quality, a willingness to be burned at the stake to obtain for a loved one the medical care needed or some service essential to his welfare. Alternative methods of securing funds were sometimes rejected or not explored. Under these circumstances, the woman's basic problem appeared to be her inability or unwillingness to permit anyone else to assume the obligations she had been conditioned to believe were inherent in the role she had assumed.

None of these women appeared to have been exposed to any group definitions of situations in which crime is appropriate or to have any experience with criminal ideology. Instead, they seemed to have been conditioned by childhood training, early education, adolescent fantasy, and adult group definitions of expected maternal or wifely behavior to feel that any conduct, including trust violation, is justified when it appears to offer the only available solution to problems seriously affecting the welfare or potential loss of a child or husband.

After their apprehension and conviction, most of these women expressed: great regret of any harm they had caused their employers or their own families; a conviction that they had no choice under the circumstances; a belief that their incarceration was justified; and some expectation that others would understand why they felt it necessary to sacrifice their positions and their potentiality for future employment in a position of trust.

### Romantic Dreamers

The characteristics and behavior of women who were Romantic Dreamers closely resembled those of the women impelled to protect the health or welfare of a loved person. One basic difference was evident: these women were not primarily concerned with the real needs of significant persons (for example, a need for medical care).

Instead, they sought either to preserve for themselves what they considered their most important possession – a husband's love, or to enhance a relationship with a lover or relative. To meet their own emotional needs they had come to believe that the desired one-to-one relationships could be achieved, retained, or regained through money available to them only through violation of their trusted positions. Like the Obsessive Protectors, these women had also been conditioned to believe that preservation of a relationship with a beloved person justified any necessary sacrifice of personal values or positions of trust.

## Greedy Opportunists

Greedy Opportunists shared many of the characteristics and motivations of those driven to violate trust by conditions jeopardizing the welfare of significant persons or their relationship with such persons. Most of these women began their illegal activities to meet similar financial needs, but became addicted to the good life after discovering the ease with which they could obtain other people's money. As one woman described the process: "Stealing became like a disease . . . and I was hooked like a dope fiend." All of these women possessed superior intelligence, but appeared to have been seduced by their success in meeting an initial financial need. Like some of the men in Cressey's study, these women seemed to "become criminals without intending to do so."

## Victims of Pressure or Persuasion

The women who were Victims of Pressure or Persuasion accepted positions of trust in good faith, but subsequently violated that trust in response to some form of pressure exerted by another person. In one instance, the motivating pressure assumed the form of persuasion, instruction, and the example of a fellow employee intent on buying protection for her own embezzlement. In others, the coercive demands or fear-inspiring threats of a husband or lover provided the impetus for criminal behavior.

Unlike the other "honest" women, these women did not embark upon their criminal activities on their own initiative. Nevertheless, their motivation partly resembled that of the Obsessive Protectors and the Romantic Dreamers. They, too, were impelled to violate trust through fear of the loss of a significant person, or a belief that a satisfying relationship would be irreparably damaged if they did not comply with a request for funds in excess of their legitimate earnings, or did not follow the example of another person with superior power.

The behavior of the "honest" women who succumbed to pressure differed from that of the Reluctant Offenders (those who intended to steal or defraud) in two important ways (see Chapter 8). In all instances, the "honest" women had held positions of trust for long periods of time (7 to 25 years) and had not taken any prior advantage of their opportunity to secure money illegally. More significantly, these women accepted full responsibility for devising ways to obtain money fraudulently and for implementing their plans. In carrying out their criminal activities, they had no crime partners even though other persons provided the motivation for their crimes.

## OTHER CONCEPTS AND TYPOLOGIES

Although this phase of the study was directed primarily toward an examination of Cressey's findings, it is appropriate to consider briefly the relevance of some other sociological concepts.

In the subgroups identified, we have seen examples of Lombroso's belief that female offenders may commit offenses in which "vengeance plays a principal part"(12) and "greed is a moving cause,"(13) or the origin of the reluctant crime "is suggestion on the part of a lover"(14) or a "sheer excess of temptation."(15) Most significantly, the findings have substantiated Elliott's conviction that some of the crimes women commit grow out of the culture of their private world where the woman's primary concern has been "her family, her husband, her children, her home."(16)

The "honest" women in this group also tend to validate Gibbons's premise that "law-breaking behavior may arise out of some combination of situational pressures and circumstances, along with opportunities for criminality which are totally outside the actors."(17) In addition, they support his contention that their behavior is indicative of "Criminality Among Respectable Citizens,"(18) and also Cavan's belief that there are "criminals who live in a non-criminal world" and "do not regard themselves as criminals or as persons opposed to conventional moral codes."(19)

## SUMMARY

This chapter supports the concept that there are similarities and differences in both the problems faced by men and women who violate financial trust and in the rationalizations or vocabularies of adjustment through which they attempt to justify their criminal behavior. It also summarizes the characteristics and behavior of the women included in this phase of the study, and presents the first segment of the typology developed for women who embezzle or defraud.

NOTES

(1) Donald R. Cressey, A Study in the Social Psychology of Embezzlement: Other People's Money (Glencoe, Illinois: Free Press, 1953), p. 157.
(2) Ibid., p. 31.
(3) Ibid., p. 32.
(4) Ibid., p. 52.
(5) Ibid., p. 66.
(6) Ibid.
(7) Ibid., p. 30.
(8) Ibid., p. 96.
(9) Ibid., p. 97.
(10) Ibid., p. 145.
(11) Ibid., p. 146.
(12) Cesare Lombroso and William Ferrero, The Female Offender (New York: Appleton, 1900), p. 148.
(13) Ibid., p. 162.
(14) Ibid., p. 196.
(15) Ibid., p. 206.
(16) Mabel A. Elliott, Crime in Modern Society (New York: Harper & Brothers, 1952), p. 261.
(17) Don C. Gibbons, Society, Crime and Criminal Careers (Englewood Cliffs, N.J.: Prentice-Hall, 1973), pp. 300-23.
(18) Ibid.
(19) Ruth Shonle Cavan, Criminology (New York: Crowell, 1948), pp. 182-203.

# III

# WOMEN WHO INTENDED TO STEAL OR DEFRAUD

# 7

# SELECTED CASE STUDIES

The case studies in this chapter provide background information on six women convicted on charges involving a variety of felonious property offenses. The common denominator in these convictions was found to be a deliberate intent to steal or defraud.

These studies, supplemented by data derived from the total sample used in this phase of the study, provide the information needed to construct the tentative typology presented in Chapter 8.

## LEONA

From time to time, Leona's picture appeared in the Society Section, as she engaged in one of her philanthropic activities. Leona was just short of being severely prim in dress and manner, but her warm, ready smile and her apparent concern about others made her an attractive person. Surely, at no time would anyone have any doubts as to the veracity or intent of this unselfish woman.

Leona was intelligent (I.Q. of 130+) but she lacked judgment, at least in the selection of a husband. Her three disastrous marriages yielded two children of her own and three stepsons, adopted because she felt they were being badly treated by their father. Each marital failure reinforced her need for money, male companionship, and excitement. She gave up some of her charitable pursuits and turned to alcohol and gambling to soothe her ragged nerves and fill her empty, lonely life.

Although not apprehended, Leona had previously embezzled $5,000 from a doctor for whom she worked. She had altered checks, created a bookkeeping system of her own, and failed to make bank deposits. To compound these "silent" felonies, Leona borrowed $3,900 from her employer, saying that her son had impregnated a girl who was threatening suicide if she did not have an abortion. Knowing of Leona's great concern for the welfare of others and remembering her long association with charitable causes, the doctor made the loan. She gratefully accepted the money and promptly disappeared. The doctor failed to prosecute, perhaps because he could not believe that Leona was capable of such devious behavior or perhaps because, like many other victims, he could not accept his own gullibility and poor judgment of people.

At age 50, Leona became involved in her greatest theft. Her modus operandi was much the same; only the setting and the people were different. Leona had known Grace Smith for 30 years. They had met in business college, both having to reconcile themselves to secretarial training because family finances made it impossible for them to continue at the state university. From there the women traveled very separate paths, Grace going on to marry the owner and operator of one of the largest lumber companies in the state. The two remained friends, however, and so Leona confided to Grace that she needed a job, not for the support of her own family but because her sister had stolen $4,000 from her employer and would go to prison if the money were not repaid quickly. To further her own plan, Leona had resorted to sheer fabrication. Grace, shocked at her friend's news and wanting desperately to help, prevailed upon her husband to give Leona a $4,000 loan and a bookkeeping job in the plant. A position was found and Leona was duly grateful for the opportunity to begin to work off the loan that "saved my sister from the penitentiary."

In the big, lofty lumberyard office Leona was her own boss, handling the accounts of several large contractors. Most importantly, Leona was completely trusted by her employer. He was, in fact, happy to have someone his wife knew so well working with the biggest accounts in the plant.

Leona worked hard, often many hours overtime, and she was highly competent. Her suggested changes in office procedures saved the owner money – so much, in fact, that Leona shared in the plant's annual bonus, the first member of the clerical staff to do so. By the end of the first year, Leona was ready to embezzle.

Leona began by setting up two bookkeeping systems, allowing her to embezzle with little difficulty. She prepared checks for her own use, then wrote checks for the company's records. She never stole any cash, relying on the appropriation of small amounts through checks attributed to petty cash. There were few internal controls and theft was easy. The company, although doing business amounting to almost $1 million a year, did not even own a check protector!

During the first three months of theft, Leona stole almost $9,000; by the end of the first year she had appropriated over $20,000 of her employer's money. She repaid her loan of $4,000 in judiciously small amounts, and with each payment told her employer how grateful she was for his kindness. However, Leona was becoming comfortable about her situation. One moment she felt she was taking too much money and later regretted there was not more to take. She worried about becoming a compulsive thief, and it concerned her that she was stealing more than she could replace. Leona began to gamble, and lost several thousand dollars on the gambling tables before she admitted that she was only compounding her problems.

Returning to work after an especially unlucky and frustrating weekend at the casinos, Leona discovered an auditor working at her desk. Her employer seemed glad to see her and explained, almost apologetically, that the audit was routine and that the books appeared to be in good shape. Leona felt safe and busied herself preparing a copy of the inventory while waiting to resume work at her own desk. When the auditor returned in midweek, however, Leona sensed danger and committed herself to a state hospital, saying that she was suicidal and felt she could not control herself. She returned home after two weeks of hospitalization, unnerved and somewhat frantic because neither her employer nor his wife, her old friend Grace, had visited or called the hospital to inquire about her illness. She sat in her apartment then and waited with a kind of fatalistic foreboding. By the end of the week she was arrested on a count of grand theft. In two years, Leona had embezzled almost $140,000 from her benefactors.

## LEONA'S RATIONALIZATION

"I tried hard to meet other people's expectations of me when I was younger, but I seemed to be unlucky all the way around. I had three rotten marriages and began to drink a great deal. I never had enough money to live on and when I got a job in which I handled so much money I just couldn't resist stealing. Then I gambled, went to casinos, and lived differently than I ever did before. I lost track of my own mind and will. I'm especially sorry about all of this because I cheated two very good and loyal friends. I also disgraced my family, my children, and myself. No one likes to go to prison, but in my case the punishment they gave is justified. I'll never stop crying about how I hurt so many people. Never."

## JUDY

Judy spent a miserable childhood in a small Missouri town. She was treated badly by her parents, who were always at odds with each other as they continuously battled poverty and wallowed helplessless in debt. When their physical abuse and a continuing demand that she do all of the housework became intolerable, Judy would sustain herself by planning to leave home when she graduated from high school, and dreaming that she would marry well and have a happy life. On graduation day, Judy was the brightest student in the graduating class (I.Q. of 140+) and the poorest student academically. She was ill equipped at 17 to fulfill her ambitions for the good life.

Judy went to Chicago and found that she could get only menial employment. She was relegated to the kitchen once again, this time with unending stacks of unwashed dishes and the added agony of watching others dine in affluent comfort and luxury. In her hurry to change this situation, she married a man she hardly knew. The only things they had in common were frustration, mutual loneliness, and a deep anger at their lot in life. In two years the marriage was over and a child, Johnny, had been born. The furniture bought during the marriage was repossessed and child care was too expensive for Judy to afford to take another menial job. Being a public assistance client was anathema to Judy since her family had been on welfare during all of her childhood, and she vowed that this stigma would not be placed upon her son.

Judy left Chicago and settled in Los Angeles, where she met a handsome and convincing pimp and became a call girl. She took good care of Johnny during the day and hired a baby-sitter for five hours each night. Because Judy was young, beautiful, and unattached, she began to build up "a good book" and her high earnings soon allowed her to sample the kind of life she had dreamed of for so long. Despite her increase in income, however, Judy worried about the effect her prostitution might have on her son's well-being. After several years of sex by contract, Judy decided to embark upon a new career. She had become an attractively socialized person, poised, polished, and beautifully groomed. Now, in a handsome tan fall outfit, she set out at age 26 to implement a plan that would eventuate in her first clash with the law.

Judy began to live in a world of aliases, 26 in all. She attached fictitious names to numerous conditional sales contracts on thousands of dollars worth of merchandise. In rapid succession she ordered color television sets, pianos, jewelry, and other expensive luxury merchandise that were delivered to her tastefully decorated apartment in a jet-set section of town. Then, through a man she had met while hustling, she fenced the merchandise after making several payments on it. In due time, Judy would move to another part of town, assume a new alias, and purchase more merchandise by contract. The operation went flawlessly for some time. Judy was astounded that people were so impressed with her convincing manner that they allowed her to buy almost anything she asked for, sometimes with little more than her signature to guarantee payment. She became disdainful of the merchants' gullibility and self-satisfied attitude toward their "sales." She began to develop a larcenous intent that fit nicely into the impersonality of the marketplace. As a result, she was able to believe that the persons who sold merchandise to her, with so little concern about her ability to pay, deserved to run into a customer like her once in a while. Flagrantly moving from one place to another, sometimes only a block away from the apartment she had just left, Judy filled ev[illegible] inch of her home with her "purchases." Deliverymen did not seem t[illegible] question the acquisition of a piano when it was apparent that there were already six in the apartment. Television sets and radios were in such abundance that her home must have appeared to be a warehouse. Nevertheless, she experienced no problems for a long time.

The aliases were finally sifted. When Judy was arrested she did not behave at all like the affluent, poised customer she had pretended to be. When police arrived, she readily agreed to dress for the ride to the station. While supposedly getting ready for the trip, she made her way through a narrow crawl hole, and unceremoniously dropped at the feet of two officers who had anticipated that this would be the way Judy would solve the problem of being taken into custody.

## JUDY'S RATIONALIZATION

Judy's only regret was that she was caught. She felt extremely bitter that she would have to serve from two to ten years because she did not "rob anyone." She believed the court should distinguish between her deception and the ruthless acts of the armed robber who stole from individuals and backed up his intent to get their money by violence if necessary. She claimed that "all of these places [the ones she had bilked] carry risk insurance and they don't lose a dime." Judy also spoke of the miniscule operation in which she engaged as compared to the "big time" swindlers and the big corporations "that fleece people out of millions every day in the week." Her parting words were: "I know that I did wrong in society's eyes, but society is harder on little people like me than it is on the big crooks, the abortionists, the pushers, and the swindlers. . . . I'm here on five counts of grand theft. I could have stolen a couple of million dollars and not gotten such a big sentence. My next caper, if there is one, is going to be big time, baby, big time all the way."

## GRACE

Grace was creative and blatantly open about her illegal behavior. It was this quality, perhaps, that allowed her to operate as long as she did and to engage in such high-level criminality. Grace was not craftily intelligent, she was artistically endowed, articulate, and very personable. She was brought up in a big family with little social status, but she had become poised, chic, and, most importantly, plausible and beautiful. These attributes took Grace into expensive homes and gave her entrée to affluence.

Her first fraudulent act involved an interior-decorating contract she made with Mr. Parrish, a wealthy businessman. Grace had come to him highly recommended by an acquaintance for whom she had done an exquisite room. Her fee had been exorbitant and her materials high priced, but there had been no dishonesty in the first transaction. Mr. Parrish, however, did not fare so well. Grace required a $5,000 retainer fee and promptly disappeared, doing none of the work she had contracted to do.

Grace was not too clear about the years between her twenty-eighth and thirty-fifth birthdays. She married once, but her husband "had no ambition" and did not like the ideas Grace had about making money. She wanted to get rich – real rich – and, according to Grace, her husband "was so square, he stunk." Grace moved ahead alone to bigger things. She attempted to buy a nightclub for $96,000 by issuing worthless bonds with a male accomplice who exonerated her. With her crime partner in prison, Grace next tried to finance the purchase of a $350,000 concession in a revived historical ghost town. She coupled that with buying a ranch, all without any visible funds. Grace used her own attributes instead: the open smile; the firm, warm, businesslike handshake; her knowledge of the area and the potential value of its property; and her apparent sincerity in wanting to make good investments for others.

Grace's biggest and certainly her most daring deal was her attempted sale of a United States Army installation to an out-of-state buyer who was looking for investment property. Grace told the potential buyer that she knew the owners very well and, although she did not know whether they were interested in selling, she would try to get the property for him at a good price. Grace called her client a few days later, saying she thought she had made a deal he would like. The client was delighted but in a hurry to catch a plane for home. They met at the airport to consummate the deal. Grace was left with a $35,000 check made out to her and a promissory note for Grace's fictitious owners. It was her last caper. The client's lawyer recognized the site he had just bought and payment on the check was stopped.

At age 41, Grace is still a youthful looking woman. Her beautiful black hair is done in an attractive upsweep. Her eyes are deep purple velvet and her voice is warm, seductive, and interesting. She hardly looks like an inmate of a correctional institution serving a sentence for eight counts of grand larceny and two for criminal conspiracy to commit grand theft.

## GRACE'S RATIONALIZATION

"I could be a millionaire if I could just have played it 'straight,' I inspire trust in people. They like me and, even when they know I've cheated them, they can hardly stand to have me arrested. Yes, I knew what I was doing was all dishonest and illegal, but I think the law is pretty screwy too. If a person wants to trust me with his own money and 'speculate,' he ought to be allowed to do that without my getting the book thrown at me. All of the people I supposedly cheated wanted to get something out of it too. There were promises of discounts, rebates, coercion, and bribery to sell property, and ready-made suckers to buy. Like that guy who wanted to buy the army camp property. He didn't know it belonged to the federal government, that's true, but he knew damned well that that property was worth five times the price I gave him. So he grabbed it! The whole bunch I dealt with were as larcenous as I. The only difference is, I took all the risks and landed in prison. They ended up 'the poor little old victims.' Bullshit!"

## JOSEPHINE

Josephine, aged 77, was the oldest woman in the sample. Josephine carried over a dozen aliases, her life having been a potpourri of illegal schemes and acts. In her last and most elaborate operation, she used her son Tom as her crime partner. Together they developed and executed a well-thought-out and seemingly foolproof act of fraud against the California Unemployment Insurance Fund.

Josephine, a large, imposing woman weighing over 200 pounds, and Tom, her even larger (270 pounds) but less imposing looking son, set up five fictitious businesses supposedly specializing in research and the sale of feature articles to newspapers. Each business (made up of Josephine and Tom) employed one or two fictitious employees and was properly registered as an employer subject to the Unemployment Insurance Code, and thus required to pay employment insurance taxes in accordance with the law. All reports turned in were in good order and there was no evidence of irregular practices.

Josephine and Tom covered 20 towns, using post office box numbers as addresses and collecting on 45 claims. The modus operandi suggests that mother and son shared equally in the innovative means they devised to defraud. Bogus identities and multiple social security numbers were used and they sometimes drew, simultaneously, the benefits from six claims. They simply posed as victims of layoffs in an occupation in which jobs were scarce and job openings infrequent. Josephine and Tom knew what they were doing, they knew how to do it, and the system seemed to defy detection for some time. However, they were eventually arrested and convicted on two counts of grand theft and conspiracy to commit grand theft.

Violation of the law was not new to Josephine or to Tom. She had spent a year in jail for stealing a sizable amount of money from the safe of a real estate broker for whom she had worked, and Tom had been incarcerated for draft evasion in World War II.

## JOSEPHINE'S RATIONALIZATION

"My son tried to get a job. I was retiring and when no job came forth for Tom we collected our unemployment insurance. Then we thought of going into business for ourselves and began the PARB Research Service. This meant Par Audit and Research Bureau. I would do the auditing, Tom the research.

"I made out income tax returns for clients and Tom wrote the newspaper articles. We started to work the unemployment insurance thing because we needed money badly. We had always lived well and loved to travel. We were always just about ready to quit, but it was hard to give it up."

## ANN AND POLLY

Ann's dark blue eyes were clear and warm, and her hair was a golden chestnut color. Her appearance and pleasant manner combined to convey an impression of an attractive young woman scarcely out of her teens, although she had had a twenty-seventh birthday.

Ann had come to California from Pittsburgh after graduation from high school. She was tired of the long, cold, and dirty winters, of her mother's preoccupation with the Bible and health fads, and of the six younger siblings who, like herself, had seldom seen their father sober. Ann's mother believed that God had ordained her to order miracles for others – for a fee. He had chosen her to be His intermediary, to bless concoctions of herbs mentioned in the Bible, and to make such potions into cures for various conditions ranging from ringworm to blindness. In short, Ann's mother was a quack, but she was confident of her own sanctity and considered herself "one of God's true helpers."

Ann came to California with Polly, a young woman her own age whom she had known all her life, and who in many ways had had a more stable home life than Ann. Polly, who had never known her own parents, had none of Ann's fresh beauty, but she was intelligent and her extrovertive nature somehow balanced Ann's tendency to be a loner. The two women seemingly had no desire to cultivate friends and their lives were almost solely dependent upon each other. They worked at a variety of temporary and part-time jobs, dressed very well, and made at least one trip a year to the Bahamas, the Fijis, or some other exotic place. Both drove moderately expensive sports cars and generally gave the appearance of being well-paid young career women.

Ann and Polly were highly successful at one of the bunco artist's oldest ploys, the pigeon-drop. They had worked it so often and so successfully that it apparently never occurred to either of them that it could ever fail. Ann would initiate the drop by selecting elderly women as her victims, since they seemed easier to deceive. These women, often lonely, were impressed with Ann's friendliness. She generally met her prospects in shopping centers and would begin her conversation by telling the victim that she reminded her of a teacher she once had and whom she deeply admired. Then Ann would find other things to talk about until she and the victim were met by Polly. Polly would approach them as a stranger very excited about an envelope she had just found in a nearby telephone booth. Ann would pretend to be very skeptical at first, allowing Polly to expand on the fact that the envelope contained $20,000 in cash and was addressed to someone in Cuba. Ann would then allow herself to become more involved, wanting to find the owner. Polly would explain that she had taken the money and the envelope to her boss, who said he had made inquiries and that the FBI would agree to the three of them dividing the money if they paid the taxes due the government on the money. Polly would elaborate that the FBI assumed the money was being transferred from this country to Cuba by bookies who did not want to pay the taxes on it. If they paid the taxes, nothing could keep them from becoming the rightful owners of the money.

Ann would ask many questions, showing some concern that this might not be legal, but always allowing enough encouragement so that the victim would begin to persuade her that this was really a matter of "finders keepers." Polly had the further task of explaining that her boss said each of them should put up $3,000 to demonstrate their good faith and to assure the "honest division of the money." By this time both Ann and Polly had generally engaged the victim in a willingness to participate in the deal. Ann was no longer reluctant because Polly had legitimized the situation by invoking her boss's name and the respectability of the FBI. The victim would rush to order a cashier's check from her bank to seal her good faith.

However successful the ploy had been so many times before and in so many different places, it was inevitable that the two young bunco artists would eventually meet a potential victim who was cautious. The act had gone on as usual and the victim was seemingly ready to be fleeced. However, when Ann and Polly insisted that she cash her $3,000 check, the victim said she would do so only after she had talked with Polly's boss so there could be some verification that she had indeed put up her share of the money. When it was apparent that the victim realized she was involved in a confidence game, both women fled but were apprehended a few hours later while engaged in a new drop in another part of town. Because they had been suspected of countless other drops, they were charged with three counts of grand theft and each drew a sentence of six months to five years in a correctional institution.

## ANN'S RATIONALIZATION

"I did misuse people's confidence in me and I stole from some old ladies who couldn't afford the loss. It was hard sometimes because they really believed me and liked me. But it was a way of making a real easy, good living and we didn't do anything to physically hurt anybody. They didn't have to give us their money at gunpoint; there was never any violence or threats. In a way, these ladies made themselves their own victims because they were looking for something for nothing. Some of those old gals were pretty cagey, too. I still think the one that got us caught was an undercover woman. The caper never failed before. Never once."

## POLLY'S RATIONALIZATION

"We had the drop down to a 't.' It worked good so many times. It seems crazy that anyone would ever believe such a story as I told them. But Ann was a great little actress; she was able to put herself in their place – after all, she was 'just a stranger' being approached too. No one ever could have told that she was in on it. Yes, I'm sorry that I did such dishonest things, but nobody ever 'makes' a sucker out of another person. They have to be a little shady too. No, I don't think I'll ever go back to the drop again. But where else can you make that kind of money?"

## LAURA

Laura and her husband Bill teamed with a third accomplice (Stoney) to engage in a fraudulent operation that the district attorney described as "cleverly managed, and executed; the magnitude of fraud being staggering."

Laura was 24 when she married Bill, a previously convicted con man. Bill was handsome, bright, amoral, and exceedingly businesslike in his various illegal activities. It was hard to understand how an attractive, well-reared young woman, whose father was a university professor, would become involved in Bill's illicit schemes. It just did not fit with the rigid religious upbringing of a girl from the rural South or with her antebellum manner. But Laura had been atypical since childhood. Her only sibling, Ruth, an older sister, finished college, went abroad to teach for a time, returned, and married an old college friend. Ruth had been a happy child, a well-adjusted young adult, and was now a happily married woman.

Laura had married first at age 18, just a few months after finishing high school. She described her husband as "a 30-year-old engineer, who came home from work, took a bottle of beer out of the refrigerator, and died in front of the TV, night after night."

Within two years Laura had had enough of her sleeping prince and found it easy to obtain a Mexican divorce. Shortly after that, she met Bill at a bar and fell in love immediately. She liked Bill's attitude – he was for quick money and so sure of himself it seemed very unlikely that he could ever get caught at anything. He gave Laura a sense of security she had never had before. Bill taught her how to get fake I.D.s, driver's licenses, and social security cards and how to use these documents in kiting worthless checks.

Laura was a very convincing forger; her manner was impeccable and the checks looked authentic. After two years, however, she was arrested. Because the checks were for small amounts and because restitution was made, Laura was formally charged with only two counts of grand theft and given a sentence of six months to five years in prison. Bill was not charged with anything since Laura had refused to name him as her accomplice.

Bill and Laura had previously agreed that he would not visit her at the jail pending trial, or at the prison. Instead, he would act like a hurt and incredulous deceived husband who was so deeply embarrassed by her behavior that he intended to divorce her.

Laura was released from prison after 16 months. Bill immediately told her of an illegal enterprise that was "all set up to bring in a great deal of loot." Bill explained that this was a "sure caper" and that they would be working with "an old pro" who "knew the ropes and all of the angles." However, Laura was not at all eager to become involved in anything that would tend to jeopardize her parole. For some time she refused to participate in Bill's plans. She contented herself with selling pornographic literature and cartoons through pulp magazine advertisements and the use of post office boxes to receive orders. Business was good and she could work alone except for contact with the compositors. It was not until Laura met Stoney, the "old pro," that she began to take an interest in Bill's proposed swindle. Stoney soon became more than a business partner; he became Laura's lover. Bill was aware of this relationship but refused to let his personal concerns interfere with his opportunity to work with Stoney and "make it big."

Stoney invested $150,000 in the C & C Construction Company, which had been owned and operated for a number of years by a legitimate businessman. It had been a reputable business and, when it changed ownership, the community assumed it would remain so. Under Bill and Stoney, however, the business was used for two illegal purposes: to serve as a front for a check-writing operation and to provide a base of operation where they could receive money for contracts for home repairs they never intended to make. Under the plan there was a very distinct division of labor among the trio. Stoney directed the preparation of checks and recruited a staff to cash them for a 5 percent commission. All checks were exactly the same in size, color, texture, and check protector embossment as the checks used by the original C & C Construction Company. As a result, the checks were immediately associated with the firm's former owner. Laura's responsibility in the operaiton was to make out the checks for Stoney's signature, disburse them to the men who would cash them, and pay the commission for all checks cashed. Over a period of several months, the C & C Construction Company passed worthless checks totaling more than $6,000 each week.

In the meantime, Bill, Laura, and Stoney accepted money for their home improvement services. To expand their operation they purchased two defunct building contracting firms in a nearby county. They merged the two, calling the new firm the E. Edwards Building Supplies Corporation. This company was used as a front for Stoney's big caper, the selling of house siding contracts. The same persons who cashed the bogus checks became the "home improvement experts," giving advice and cost estimates and, after the hard sell, collecting a sizable down payment. Stoney had carefully studied siding costs in each community he intended to cover and his prices were always well below those of the local competition. Stoney's salesmen assured the victims that the kind of siding they were selling was guaranteed to last for the life of the house, and it would never need to be painted – not even retouched. The company also carried its own contracts, there would be no interest charge, and an inordinately long-term payment plan was available. Homeowners found these incentives irresistible. In less than a month Stoney, his two partners, and five salesmen netted $39,000 in down payment fees. Before the E. Edwards Building Supplies Corporation moved out of the area, Laura had also typed, Stoney had signed, and the sales staff had kited about $115,000 in worthless checks.

The operatives quickly moved to another community, where they set up new home improvement contracting firms. The same operational pattern was used and the group took in $130,000 within five weeks. By this time, however, the customers who had given down payments were demanding the siding jobs for which they had contracted with the C & C and the Edwards corporations. Since both establishments had been abandoned, the aggrieved victims appealed to their district attorney. The three major thieves were soon apprehended. Bill and Stoney received maximum sentences on six counts of grand theft and conspiracy. Laura received a lesser sentence on two counts of grand theft and conspiracy.

## LAURA'S RATIONALIZATION

"We bought into the home improvement, roofing, and siding business hoping to make a good profit on our investment. My husband had had a prior [arrest] on a very foolish deal he got in on with some other people and he was anxious to clear his record and get into a legitimate business. Things would have turned out all right if it hadn't been for our partner, Stoney, who wanted to expand way beyond our means to finance the business. Then I got hopelessly involved with him, and I was so much in love it made for bad feeling between my husband and Stoney. I'm sure my husband would have left me if we weren't all in this deal together.

"We had a pretty good-sized investment but we ran out of money to buy materials to satisfy the contracts we had made. We put all of the money we got in the bank and we tried to cover our expenses, hoping that we could get bank financing. I really didn't know much about the business. My part was only to type the checks I was given; I did not sign or cash any checks. The whole thing turned out so much differently than we expected it would. We just couldn't keep on top of things. I never intended for anyone to suffer a loss or for any individual to gain. I realize now that things we did were wrong. It was morally wrong. I pleaded guilty because of this."

# 8

# INTENT TO STEAL OR DEFRAUD

The women described in this chapter had two factors in common: they had been convicted on felonies involving an intent to obtain "other people's money or services" fraudulently, and they were incarcerated at the California Institution for Women.

Most of these women were initially selected for potential inclusion in the study of women who had violated positions of trust. They were subsequently excluded from that sample when it was found that they did not meet Cressey's basic criterion – they "had not accepted a position of trust in good faith."(1) At a later point other women were added to this group when a separate exploration of credit card fraud was undertaken. In that study it soon became evident that a homogeneous pattern of criminal behavior could be identified among women previously convicted of the possession or sale of drugs. Women whose arrest records included such charges were therefore excluded from the group described in this chapter. Other women convicted of forgery involving fraudulent use of checks or credit cards remained a part of the sample examined in this chapter.

The methods used to select women with intent to defraud tend to limit the conclusions that can be drawn from this sample. Despite this fact, the data collected would seem to provide a provocative basis for further research. The sections that follow describe the offenses, characteristics, and behavior of women included in this sample; present a tentative classification of the behavior systems identified; assess the degree to which relevant concepts, classifications, and typologies cited in Chapter 2 seem applicable to women convicted of offenses involving an attempt to deceive; and conclude with a brief summary.

## TYPE OF OFFENSE

As noted in earlier chapters, there is general agreement that classification by legal offense fails to provide needed information about the person and his situation, and may give an erroneous impression that only one type of crime will be committed by persons with specified characteristics. The arrest records of women convicted of crimes reflecting an intent to steal or defraud would seem to support these premises. About 50 percent of the women in this group were convicted on charges that included grand theft. The others received prison sentences based on one or more charges of grand larceny, conspiracy to commit grand theft, forgery, possession of blank and unfinished checks, and theft of credit cards. As Cressey discovered in his study of trust violation, these charges "did not describe a homogeneous class of behavior."(2) In fact, some of these women had been convicted of crimes that differed from those previously described as "criminal violation of financial trust" only in the fact that the offenders had not "accepted a position of trust in good faith" (see Leona's case study in Chapter 7).

Nearly 60 percent of the women with intent to defraud had no prior arrest record. This fact appeared to have no relation to the duration of their criminal careers or to the nature of their offense patterns. Some women had played the same confidence game in countless communities from coast to coast, with no prior arrests (for example, Polly and Ann). Other women had engaged in a wide variety of illegal efforts to defraud, but had only one prior arrest (Laura, Grace, and Josephine). Others with similar behavior patterns had had as many as ten prior convictions (for example, Gloria). For some women, legally prohibited activities had been interspersed with legitimate employment (Josephine), but for others law violation had become a way of life. For a few women, arrest and conviction had followed their first ventures into the world of fraud (Eve).

Despite the legal nomenclature used as a basis for conviction, the actual offenses committed by these women ranged from embezzlement of funds (maximum amount $140,000) through a wide variety of confidence games that included the traditional pigeon-drop, the sale of federal land, and the fraudulent use of charge accounts, to the forgery of checks, money orders, and credit cards with and without prior theft of the instruments used to obtain money fraudulently.

## TENTATIVE TYPOLOGY

The approaches used by Lemert and Conklin provide useful ways of examining the criminal behavior of women convicted of offenses involving a deliberate attempt to obtain money or services through false pretenses. Their findings will be reviewed in Chapter 9. It is important to note here only the similarities and differences in their efforts to order a mass of diverse data.

In his early study of 75 persons serving sentences for check forgery, Lemert: identified three groups with different sets of self-perceptions, techniques, and life organization; excluded from his sample the group for whom forgery "was simply an aspect of alcoholism, gambling or one of a series of criminal offenses having little or no consistency"(3); established criteria for classification as "a systematic check forger"; compared the characteristics and behavior of inmates who met these criteria with the typology of professional theft formulated by Sutherland; and "concluded that present day check forgery exists in systematic form,"(4) but its characteristics are different from those described by Sutherland.

Conklin's report of his study of 67 men convicted of robbery: identified four types of offenders by basing classification on "motivation for theft, techniques used and the degree of individual commitment to crime as a way of life"(5); compared this typology with those developed by several students of robbery and other forms of theft, including Sutherland; examined, in some detail, three components of the offender's decision to commit a theft (decision that he must have more money, selection of a target, and planning of the crime)(6); and concluded that each type of offender has "a different reason for wanting money, a different technique for committing a robbery and a different degree of commitment to crime."(7) Unlike Lemert, he did not exclude from consideration the alcoholic "whose commitment to theft is weak and short-lived,"(8) or the drug addict whom we have elected to describe in a separate chapter. Instead, "the alcoholic robber" and the "addict robber" are presented as two of his four offender categories.

The samples used by Lemert and Conklin differed from the group of women described in this chapter in one important way. All offenders included in Lemert's sample (8 women and 67 men) had been convicted of the same crimes – check forgery and writing checks with insufficient funds. Likewise, all men in Conklin's sample had been sentenced for the crime of robbery, which by definition involved the use of force as well as the theft of property.(9) In our attempt to identify a homogeneous class of behavior comparable to that described by Cressey as "criminal violation of trust," we have again grouped together women whose behavior seemed to possess common denominators and to disregard what appeared to be more or less accidental differences in the criminal charges on which their convictions were based. Efforts to identify common threads in motivation, self-perception, value systems, modus operandi, life-style and organization, and "degree of individual commitment to crime as a way of life" produced a typology that reflects, in part, the offender's emotional or attitudinal response to her life experiences and to any current pressure or persuasion exerted by significant others.

This typology does not purport to include all women who engage in fraudulent activities. Instead, it is based on data obtained from the sample selected as previously described. It may consequently be skewed by the sampling methods used, as well as by the non-scientific selection process through which police decided which women should be arrested and courts made decisions as to whether a convicted woman should be placed on probation, given a brief jail sentence, or sent to the state correctional facility.

Because these women used widely differing techniques and their convictions were based on a variety of legal charges, the descriptive terms coined to denote the three subtypes identified make no reference to a legal offense. Instead,these labels were chosen to indicate, for each behavior system described, the offenders' emotional or attitudinal approach to crime, their perception of their roles in the crimes committed, and their relationship to their crime partners or to the world in general.

## The Vindictive Self-Servers

The Vindictive Self-Servers are women who believed that: their life experiences entitled them to some compensation for their childhood deprivation or adult hardships ("the world owes me a better life than I have had"); and the acquisition of money or goods by illegal means is therefore a defensible actor method of earning a livelihood.

Their offense patterns appeared to have no commonality beyond the fact that none of the women assigned to this category had any prior arrest record. Like Conklin's "opportunist robbers," they seemed likely to choose targets for "their accessibility and vulnerability," (10) but here the resemblance ceased. In most instances, their intelligence was high – an I.Q. of 130 to 140 – and their modus operandi was based on a planned use of whatever skills, talents, or natural attributes were in thier possession, such as bookkeeping skills, imagination, poise and beauty or an appealing and trustworthy appearance.

Their self-concepts in terms of criminality were not wholly apparent, nor was the duration of their future criminal careers predictable. In some instances, it seemed probable that their hostility about the cruelty of fate, fury over their arrest and conviction, and some prior association with the criminal world would propel them into a fully developed criminal career (for example, Judy). In others, the criminal acts committed might well represent a cry for help, an effort to punish significant persons for their neglect or cruel treatment, or a need for self-punishment. Conceivably, women with these motivations might follow the pattern of Gibbons's "one-time loser property offender [who] commits isolated acts of petty or major larceny"(11) with no recurrence of illegality. His classification would not be appropriate, however, because some women in this group embezzled their employer's funds, and Gibbons elected to exclude from this class the embezzler whom he considered to be an example of "criminality among respectable citizens."(12).

The acquisition of money or goods was an immediate objective in all cases but, for most women in this group, it did not appear to constitute a primary motive for theft. Instead, they seemed impelled toward some action that would provide an emotional outlet for pent-up feelings of loneliness, envy, frustration, disillusionment, or self-pity. Like Cressey's "absconders," some of these women appeared "to conclude that their attempts to conduct their lives on an honest basis have been futile, [ and ] that they don't care what happens to them"(13) – a hedonistic attitude, "eat, drink, and be merry for tomorrow you die." Others seem to display the quality of vengeance identified by Lombroso so long ago.

Unlike Conklin's "opportunist robbers," age did not seem to be a significant factor because the age range extended from 22 to 50 years. Marital status seemed to be the only factor held in common: all of the women in this group had one or more unsuccessful marriages and were currently living alone, with a child or children, or with their parents. Their marital disruption and social isolation seemed to resemble those of Lemert's "naive check forger," but none of these women had used check forgery as a means of finding relief from situational tension. (14)

The wide range of offenses, peer associations, and patterns of life organization becomes apparent in the following vignettes.

Leona

Leona embarked upon a game plan designed to facilitate the embezzlement of large sums of money (see case study). This was the second vindictive caper Leona had directed toward employers whose wives had everything she failed to obtain or maintain. Her search for vengeance or some feeling of power over the people in her life is perhaps most evident in the bizarre tales she concocted for use in obtaining a job or a loan from her employers. Her free-floating hostility is also indicated by an apparent wish to damage the reputations of her son and sister as she proceeded on her self-serving way.

Unlike most of the "honest" women who violated trust, Leona seemed to have no financial problems that could not be solved by legal means. In fact, fictional problems were invented unnecessarily as she carefully designed and implemented her plans to appropriate her employer's money. Although she worried at one point about her inability to replace the large amounts taken from her last employer, it seemed probable that this concern provided a rational for her return to gambling and not for termination of her swindling activities. Certainly she could not be classified as "a naive check forger," but her criminal pattern appeared to demonstrate the same need for "closure" in relief of tension identified by Lemert in his study of check forgery.(15)

Leona spent many weekends at gambling tables, but there is no indication that she had any close association with professional criminals. Evidence of commitment to crime as a way of life is also lacking. Her fears about becoming a compulsive thief do indicate a realization that, like Cressey's embezzlers, she had "slipped into a category [criminal] which . . . is regarded as undesirable" and that, like them, she became "extremely nervous, tense, emotionally upset and unhappy." The result was that she behaved in a "rather incongruous fashion"(16) when she realized that her embezzlement would be detected in the annual audit.

Eve

Eve was one of several women whose brief criminal career seemed to express both a cry for help and a vindictive need to punish. Eve was the youngest woman in this group (22 years) and, with an I.Q. of 112, the least intelligent. As a juvenile, she had run away from home because both parents worked and she was lonely. Later she attempted a marriage that failed after the death of twin infants. When she discovered that she was pregnant again she returned to her parents' home and subsequently released her baby for adoption. In her loneliness she then set in motion a strange chain of events. By some means never explained, she came into possession of a Master Charge card issued in the name of another woman. Eve first used it to obtain a $43 engine tune-up for her car. She then began a series of weekly visits to a tire firm after inquiring whether credit cards were acceptable.

She rolled the first tire purchased down the street, and in the following week asked that a second tire be placed in the trunk of the car. By this time, the credit card had been reported lost or stolen and, when she returned asking that two more tires be placed in her car, she was apprehended. Because the court was intent on discouraging the fraudulent use of credit cards at that time, she received a prison sentence for what was, in effect, her first criminal offense.

There was no evidence that Eve had had any contacts with other offenders or that she thought of herself as a criminal. Instead, she seemed to be immersed in self-pity and determined to punish her parents and possibly her former husband by disgracing the family.

Judy

Judy developed a deep anger against her lot in life while she was a child in a family warped by poverty (see case study). Her use of fraudulent charge accounts to secure possession of expensive merchandise resembled closely the techniques employed by women engaged in various types of confidence games. The essential difference appeared to lie in the depth of anger centered around her arrest and the terms of her sentence. To her, the plan she had devised was not a game but a means of survival in the manner to which she felt entitled by virtue of her thwarted dreams and unrewarding life. Although she recognized her violation of societal norms, it seemed evident that her life experiences and associations had eroded her value system and enabled her to believe that theft from business firms, like prostitution, was a victimless crime.

## Asocial Entrepreneurs

Asocial Entrepreneurs are women who: engaged in fraudulent activities as if they were legitimate business enterprises; assumed full responsibility for planning and executing their illegal schemes or shared such responsibility with a coequal partner; and tended to justify their criminal behavior by equating their activities to those of legitimate business entrepreneurs or by citing the larcenous desires of their victims.

The arrest records of these women showed no consistency in prior convictions, duration of criminal behavior, or modus operandi. Only one-third in this category had been arrested previously, but these prior offenders had been convicted of property offenses on one to ten occasions. The existence or absence of prior arrest records seemed to have little or no relation to the duration of criminal behavior.

The methods used to acquire money or goods to which these women had no legal right ranged from traditional confidence games (for example, the pigeon-drop), through an elaborate bookkeeping operation designed to permit the collection of fraudulent claims for unemployment insurance (Josephine), to a variety of misrepresentations made in the course of what purported to be legitimate business. Like some Vindictive Self-Servers, a few of these women could prove to be "one-time losers," but with their personal characteristics, attitudes, and philosophical approach to life, it seemed probable that the majority would become, or continue to be, occasional property offenders or career criminals.

Once again, age appeared to have no significance as the age range extended from 21 to 77 years. These women were usually high school or college graduates, all had normal or superior intelligence, and a high proportion either had never married or had no intact marriage at the time of their arrest. Women with children tended to be atypical.

As the subtype designation implies, all these women had been engaged in a planned effort to "obtain something for nothing." They also had in common an identifiable constellation of skills, attitudes, personal characteristics, and motivational factors. Like the confidence men so frequently discussed in the literature, the majority were proud of their ability to inspire trust, to manipulate people, and to live by their wits. In some instances, however, their criminal activities did not meet the criteria usually considered to "distinguish the practice of confidence from other types of fraud."(17) In Gasser's opinion:

> the controlling factor in all true confidence schemes is the way in which the victim is involved. . . . Their common element is showing the victim how to make money, or gain some other advantage, in a dishonest manner and then taking advantage of his dishonesty.(18)

Instead, the fraudulent schemes developed by several women in this group were designed to defraud governmental programs, while others involved the theft of funds entrusted to firms that the victims believed to be legitimate business enterprises (such as an escrow company).

It is interesting to note that all women in this class appeared to share the philosophy of life characteristic of confidence men. In essence, the majority seemed to believe that all persons are dishonest or the use they made of their talent did not differ in any significant way from that displayed by other people in business for themselves.(19)

Most of the women also exhibited other attitudes and behavior frequently attributed to confidence men or professional thieves.(20) Although the acquisition of money or goods was important, the basic allure of their nefarious schemes often seemed to stem from the excitement and ego-rewarding thrill of the chase, the sense of power derived from the use of their wits or the manipulation of their victims, and the sheer enjoyment of playing a part in a scenario wholly unrelated to the real world in which they lived. Like the confidence men studied by Blum, many of these women were

> busy acting out their fantasied desires to be (more accurately to appear to others to be) persons of importance . . . repetitively "proving" their cleverness and superiority . . . and constantly demonstrating that they did not "grow up with a proper conscience."(21)

Unlike the men in his study, however, these women did not indicate any need to project

> the image of "the big spender" for whom money is important only in so far as one demonstrates one's worth in its spending . . . and . . . shows oneself to be a "swinger" . . . that is, a generous risk-taking, pleasure-loving, free and easy sort of chap.(22)

This disparity may well be attributed to differences in sex roles since, in our culture, the role of the expansive big spender is not one customarily assumed by women. In a more pragmatic way, the women assigned to this category seemed motivated primarily by a self-rewarding desire to acquire through any means available to them the luxurious creature comforts to which they asired, such as good cars, travel, or comfortable living quarters.

None of the women in this group denied their crime or their intent to defraud. Those who had engaged in typical confidence games invariably used some form of the rationalization common to confidence men – "the victim's greed . . . is to blame for succumbing to the blandishments of the con games."(23) A few women who had developed skill in the use of the pigeon-drop (Polly) verbalized some regret that they had enticed "old ladies who couldn't afford the loss," but quickly shrugged off any incipient guilt in true sociopathic manner (see case study).

Women who had developed other fraudulent schemes also indicated no remorse. Like the women who played the confidence games, their only real regret seemed to center around the fact that they had been arrested. Those with prior arrest records usually accepted their most recent conviction as a natural hazard associated with this means of earning a livelihood. Conversely, those with no prior arrest records either seemed confounded by what had "gone wrong" in this particular caper or were resentful that they had been sentenced to prison for law violations that they considered to be minor transgressions.

A majority of the women in this group seemed to identify themselves with a career criminal role, but there was no direct evidence of any association with criminals other than their crime partners. About 60 percent of the women in this group had crime partners, usually a husband, son, or female associate. For first offenders not engaged in confidence games there seemed to be no reason to suspect that criminal associations had been formed. It seems unlikely, however, that anyone could have mastered so successfully the techniques and skills used in the pigeon-drops without an experienced tutor. In this connection it may be of interest to note that none of the other confidence game scenarios described by Blum(24) was used by the women in this subtype. The nature of the fraudulent activities designed by these women and the attitudes they brought to their crimes are evident in the following summaries.

Grace

Grace presents an excellent example of the Asocial Entrepreneur engaged in "the chronic violation of a wide range of criminal laws . . . [usually] property crimes . . . with disregard for ordinary interpersonal conventions."(25) Like the typical confidence man, she saw no reason for laws that protect people as larcenous as she, and gloried in her ability to inspire trust in people who want o speculate (see case study).

Reared in a large family with few material benefits, Grace appears to have become enamored of her own beauty, intelligence, ability to create rewarding interpersonal relationships, and desire to acquire great wealth quickly. There is no evidence that Grace was inducted into the criminal world by other professional thieves.

Gloria

Gloria (age 33; I.Q. of 120) had ten prior arrests involving charges ranging from violation of probation to grand theft and false entry in the records of a federal credit institution. Gloria was the only woman in this group who had an intact marriage at the time of her arrest. Her last conviction was based on a charge of grand theft ($25,000) from her employer, a savings and loan association, but she and her husband had previously set up their own escrow company, made false loans, and misappropriated funds entrusted to them pending completion of various financial transactions. On one occasion she had been returned to prison because she had violated parole by failing to report her involvement in a business enterprise. Although her husband had acted as her crime partner in the escrow venture, it was evident that Gloria was the chief facilitator and was motivated primarily by a need for money and status.

Josephine

Josephine also had a crime partner in her most recent offense, but it was her son who helped her establish five fictitious business enterprises (see case study). Although Josephine had only one prior arrest (for embezzlement), her illegal activities had apparently extended over many decades and had been interspersed with legitimate employment as an accountant.

Ann and Polly

Ann and Polly seemed typical of the women who develop skill in the execution of traditional confidence games (see case study). Ann's induction into fraudulent activities may have had a direct relationship to her childhood experiences. Like the confidence men included in Roebuck's study, she grew up in a home in which there was "early reliance . . . on deceit as a major tool of life"(26) and "an early necessity for the practice, support and reward of deceit."(27) Although her mother's quackery as a religious fanatic was of a different order, certainly the mother's performance of miracles for a fee would tend to inhibit a daughter's development of a proper conscience, and thus encourage Ann's subsequent misuse of the confidence she had learned to inspire in her pigeon-drop activities.

### Reluctant Offenders

Reluctant Offenders are women who: committed various property offenses, such as forgery, credit card fraud, and possession of blank and unfinished checks; assumed little or no responsibility for planning or initiating their criminal activities; and claimed they were enticed or forced to engage in specified illegal acts by a husband or paramour.

All women in this group had prior arrest records, but the majority had not been sentenced to prison after earlier convictions. In most instances, their continuance of criminal careers seemed probable because there was no evidence that they would be less influenced by a controlling male in the future.

The majority of these women had children and all were living with legal or common-law husbands. Over 60 percent of these men were engaged in some criminal activity in which they expected their wives to fulfill assigned roles. The other men apparently depended upon their wives to supply funds for basic maintenance or supplementary support, dictated the kind of criminality from which their income would be derived, and sometimes enforced their demands through beatings or other forms of physical or emotional pressure.

Basically, the women in this group resembled those described by Lombroso and Ferrero when they identified the female offenders who "steal or compromise themselves for men's sake without having sometimes any direct interest in the act."(28) In some ways, too, they seemed similar to the "honest" women who violated trust when faced with problems "involving pressure or persuasion by a significant person," as described in Chapter 6. Probably the only essential difference between these two categories is that the trust violators, by definition, had accepted their positions of trust with no criminal intent.

Although all women assigned to this subtype had normal intelligence, the Reluctant Offenders did not include any women of superior intellect. Their I.Q.s ranged from 101 to 120. The age range (25 to 37 years) was also less extensive than that of other subtypes in this class. By accident, perhaps, no women in this sample had a marketable skill that could produce legitimately enough income to meet the demands of their husbands or lovers.

All women in this group appeared to undertake criminal behavior reluctantly. Approximately one-third did so to retain the love of their husbands or lovers. The others seemed to respond primarily to threats or acts of violence, although some of the latter group eventually learned to use, for their own benefit, the fraudulent behavior demanded by their husbands. The following summaries may clarify the interpersonal relations, motivations, and modus operandi characteristic of this type of criminality:

Tillie

Tillie, aged 37, had an I.Q. of 109. Her life became particularly difficult after her husband became obsessed with the idea that she could supplement their income through the theft and fraudulent use of credit cards. At the time of the study, Tillie was serving a sentence of six months to 14 years received on two counts of credit card forgery. This was her first prison term but she had seven prior convictions. On one occasion she was arrested with her husband after a neighbor tried to intervene when her husband was beating her because she was not stealing enough to satisfy him. While her husband was in jail she was able to obtain employment in the Head Start Program. After his release, her husband forced her to give it up. He claimed the $400 a month salary was so small that she could get more money stealing and forging credit cards.

Mae

Mae, 26 years old with an I.Q. of 101, was an obese, pregnant woman at the time of her last arrest. She had never married but had one child, three-and-one-half years old, by a former lover. She and her current common-law husband had been engaged in a complicated illegal operation that included the theft and fraudulent use of blank checks, money orders, credit cards, and driver's licenses. Because her lover was on parole after serving a prison term on forgery charges, Mae became his reluctant tool. Mae's accounts of their activities were somewhat bizarre, but it seemed evident that he had taken responsibility for stealing the forms and documents she used to obtain money fraudulently.

Mae had one prior arrest on forgery charges but had been released on probation. Her sentence to prison was based on charges that included violation of probation, six counts of forgery involving 21 checks in the total amount of $2,788, and two counts of possession of blank and unfinished checks and money orders. One hundred and twelve checks had been stolen from the owner's car. The credit cards and driver's license used for identification came from a stolen purse, and the money orders and checks from other business firms were acquired by unknown means.

When arrested, Mae attempted suicide by taking 22 seconal tablets. At the time of the study, she claimed that she was glad that she was apprehended because otherwise she "would have gone on to bigger crimes." She explained that she had agreed to forge the checks her lover provided because she could not find a job and did not want to apply for public assistance. Her lover was not arrested because he had threatened to kill her if she did not "take the rap" for the whole operation.

Laura

Laura was not forced into her subsidiary illegal role. Instead, she became the "reluctant tool" of two career criminals in a much more complicated manner (see case study).

Laura's marriage to a convicted con man appeared to have been motivated by some need to punish her university professor father and her conforming, and always approved, older sister. Unlike the Vindictive Self-Servers, however, she assumed little or no responsibility for planning or initiating her own illegal activities.

Laura's first prison experience seemed to interrupt her progress toward a criminal career. After her release Laura, like some of Cressey's trust violators, seemed impelled to make some effort to regain "membership in a social order which condemns crime and considers honesty as an ideal."(29) At first, she refused to participate in her husband's plan to undertake a large swindling operation. Her resolve was partially eroded, however, when she fell in love with her husband's new crime partner. Her new infatuation apparently made it impossible for her to refuse to accept some role in his fraudulent activities. Like Cressey's trust violators who "kidded themselves" into believing they were only "borrowing" their clients' money, Laura seemed able to reconcile her criminal behavior with her rediscovered noncriminal value system by: limiting her own activities to the typing and distribution of checks; maintaining a pervasive ignorance about the true nature of the business enterprises operated by her crime partners; and convincing herself that "her husband was anxious to clear his record and get into a legitimate business." When the trio was apprehended, Laura pleaded guilty to two counts of grand theft and conspiracy and was returned to the correctional institution. At the time of the study, her remorse and self-recrimination were similar to those of "the honest women who violated trust" described in Chapter 5. Whether she would, in fact, "return to membership in a social order which condemns crime" or become a career criminal when released from prison seemed unpredictable.

## SUMMARY

This chapter identifies the classes of behavior among the women who intended to steal or defraud, and examines briefly the approaches used in developing two typologies that appear to have some relevance to the data produced in this phase of the study. In Chapter 9, this material forms a basis for the conclusions reached as other typologies are reviewed.

NOTES

(1) Donald R. Cressey, A Study in the Social Psychology of Embezzlement: Other People's Money (Glencoe, Ill.: Free Press, 1953), p. 20.

(2) Ibid., p. 19.

(3) Edwin M. Lemert, "The Behavior of the Systematic Check Forger," Social Problems 6 (Fall 1958): 141.

(4) Ibid., p. 148.

(5) John D. Conklin, Robbery and the Criminal Justice System (Philadelphia: Lippincott, 1972), p. 59.

(6) Ibid., p. 79.

(7) Ibid., p. 182.

(8) Ibid.

(9) Ibid., p. 5.

(10) Ibid., p. 68.

(11) Don C. Gibbons, Society, Crime and Criminal Careers (Englewood Cliffs, N.J.: Prentice-Hall, 1973), p. 320.

(12) Ibid., pp. 341-42.

(13) Cressey, Other People's Money, p. 128.

(14) Edwin M. Lemert, "An Isolation and Closure Theory of Naive Check Forgery," Journal of Criminal Law, Criminology and Police Science 44 (September-October 1953): 304-5.

(15) Ibid.

(16) Cressey, Other People's Money, p. 121.

(17) Robert Louis Gasser, "The Confidence Game," Federal Probation 27 (December 1963): 47-54.

(18) Ibid.

(19) Marshall B. Clinard and Richard Quinney, Criminal Behavior Systems, A Typology (New York: Holt, Rinehart and Winston, 1973), p. 250.

(20) Herbert A. Bloch and Gilbert Geis, Man, Crime and Society (New York: Random House, 1962), p. 200.

(21) Richard H. Blum, Deceivers and Deceived (Springfield, Ill.: Charles C. Thomas, 1972), p. 13.

(22) Ibid.

(23) Ibid., p. 15.

(24) Ibid., pp. 257-320.

(25) Ibid., p. 13.

(26) Julian B. Roebuck, Criminal Typology (Springfield, Ill.: Charles C. Thomas, 1967), p. 183.

(27) Ibid., p. 198.

(28) Cesare Lombroso and William Ferrero, The Female Offender (New York: Appleton, 1900), p. 196.

(29) Cressey, Other People's Money, p. 123.

# 9

# CONCLUSIONS

This chapter will: present a composite of the total sample of women who intended to steal or defraud; examine the extent to which classifications developed by other authors seem applicable to these women; and summarize the findings in this phase of the study.

## COMPOSITE PROFILE: WOMEN WHO INTENDED TO STEAL OR DEFRAUD

The women serving sentences involving a felonious intent to steal or defraud usually had the following characteristics.

### Normal or Superior Intelligence

More than one-third of the women in this sample had I.Q.s in excess of 120, although the range extended from 101 to 140.

### Attractive or Trustworthy Appearance

Women convicted on charges involving confidence games were generally endowed with physical beauty or were imposing in appearance. A capacity to inspire trust was a common characteristic, but excess weight detracted from the appearance of several women convicted of forgery. Age did not appear to be a significant factor, although the majority were less than 30 years of age (age range, 22 to 77 years).

### High School Education or More

Most of the women had completed high school and approximately 25 percent had attended college or a business college.

### Limited Occupational Competence

These women usually had no education, training, or prior employment that would qualify them for any legal employment of a lucrative nature. The sample did include two bookkeepers and several others whose intelligence and appearance certainly would have enabled them to succeed in some legitimate enterprise.

### Unstable Employment Record

With the exception of two bookkeepers, none of these women had any record of sustained employment in a legally approved occupation. Any employment of this kind had been brief and most women had never held a job of any kind.

### No Currently Existing Marriage

Seventy-five percent of these women had been married at the time of their arrest. The husbands of women in this group had served as their crime partners or allegedly had forced them to commit the crimes for which they were apprehended.

A majority (66 percent) had children, but only one-third had children living in the home at the time of their arrest.

### No Significant Status in Parental Family

No defined trend in family constellation or in order of birth was evident. One-third of the women came from large families (a minimum of six children) in which poverty, alcoholism, and physical abuse had been factors contributing to early departure from their parental homes. Marked disparity in the socioeconomic status of parental families was apparent – Laura's father was a university professor and Ann's mother was a quack miracle healer attempting to supplement the income of an alcoholic husband.

### No Consistent Pattern of Prior Arrests

Nearly 60 percent had no prior convictions. Others had one to ten arrests.

## OTHER CLASSIFICATIONS AND TYPOLOGIES

Chapter 2 describes in some detail an array of scholarly efforts isolate for study particular types of criminal behavior that involve offenses against property. As indicated in that chapter, the typologies developed are usually based on an assumption that sex differences are not reflected in criminal behavior, or that any existing differences would have little significance because the number of women included in any sample would be small. It seems important, therefore, to compare the findings in this study with some of the criminal behavior systems described by authors primarily concerned with the behavior of male offenders.

## The Professional Thief

As previously stated, many criminologists (such as Akers and Clinard and Quinney) still insist that terms reflecting the concept of crime as a profession be reserved for offenders who approximate the criteria listed by Sutherland in The Professional Thief.(1) Because the norms and values of a profession exert a significant impact on the behavior and self-concept of its members, it may be useful to review the characteristics and behavior of women with intent to defraud to determine, if possible, the presence or absence of factors that would entitle them to be considered members of a profession.

### A Complex of Technical Skills

Sutherland specifically listed skills necessary "to the planning and execution of crime, the disposal of stolen goods, the fixing of cases in which arrests occur and the control of other situations which may arise in the course of the occupation." He identified as the "principal elements in these techniques . . . wits, [front] and talking ability."(2)

All the women described in this category possessed the techniques needed to perform the crimes undertaken, but the Reluctant Offenders assumed little or no responsibility for planning these crimes. With one exception, none of these women had any need to develop skills essential to the disposition of stolen goods.

Because these women had been sentenced to prison, it seems obvious that they lacked the skills necessary to control the situation that led to their apprehension or to fix their cases when arrests occurred. Sutherland believed that the latter techniques could be acquired "only in association with professional thieves"(3) and with their cooperation. The absence of such ties may well explain the arrests of some women who operated as loners or as a tightly knit duo with a husband, lover, son, or female associate. It is also evident, however, that arrest-preventing skill had not been acquired by the women who did have some association with career criminals.

## Status

Sutherland concluded that: high status is enjoyed by the professional thief; his prestige is based on "his technical skill, financial standing, connections, power, dress, manners and wide knowledge required in his migratory life"; and his status can be seen in "the attitudes of other criminals, the police, the court officials, newspapers and others."(4)

There is little evidence that any of the women in this sample had acquired prestige in the criminal world or with law enforcement officials. It seems probable that the appearance, dress, manners, and expensive cars of women successful in confidence games helped them to gain the trust of their victims, but there is no indication that the criminal world was impressed by these attributes. Even when some criminal associations were indicated, it seems unlikely that the status of a professional had been gained. This assumption would seem valid because persons using the pigeon-drop stand low in the hierarchy of confidence personnel,(5) and a similar status is assigned to women who act as tools for career criminals.

## Consensus

Sutherland defined the profession of theft as "a complex of common and shared feelings, sentiments and overt acts" that enable thieves to work together, culminate "in similar and common reaction to the law, which is regarded as the common enemy," and from which "develop the codes, the attitudes of helpfulness, and the loyalties of the underworld."(6)

The only women whose behavior, attitudes, and values provided any semblance of conformity with this criterion were the Asocial Entrepreneurs who had been involved in confidence games of some type. All these women expressed the rationalizations characteristic of professional confidence men (their victims were equally dishonest), and the majority regarded the law as their enemy.

Some of the women classified as Vindictive Self-Servers regarded as enemies the law and those employed to enforce it, but these women seemed equally hostile toward more successful members of the criminal world. The Reluctant Offenders did not feel any identification with criminals, and therefore did not feel any identification with "the values and esprit de corps which support the professional thief in his criminal career."(7)

## Differential Association

Sutherland believed that the final definition of the professional thief is found in the essential requirement that a professional thief be recognized and accepted as such by a group of professional thieves. In his words, "One who is not so received and recognized is not a professional thief, regardless of his methods of making a living."(8)

Available data are not conclusive, but it seems unlikely that any of the women in this study would be considered professional by a group of career criminals. In time, one woman may achieve that status if she chooses a professional mentor to prepare for the "big caper." The modus operandi that resulted in her first conviction certainly would not earn her the respect of professional thieves, even though she did have the cooperation of a fence in the disposition of stolen goods.

Most of the women who intended to defraud maintained contact with a noncriminal world and "had consensus with the larger society in regard to many of the values of the larger society,"(9) especially in "their interest in money and in the things that money will buy."(10) There is no indication, however, that any of these women received "assistance from persons in agencies which are regarded as legitimate or as official protectors of legitimate society," such as politicians, police, and the courts.(11)

## Organization

Sutherland pulled together under the heading of organization the concepts he had previously listed. He concluded that professional theft is organized crime in the sense that: "it is a system in which informal unity and reciprocity may be found"(12); it has a body of knowledge that "becomes common property of the profession"(13); and it is "a group way of life in which selection and tutelage are the two necessary elements in the process of acquiring recognition as a professional thief."(14)

As previously indicated, it seems evident that some of the women who intended to defraud could meet one or more of the criteria through which Sutherland identified the behavior system of professional thieves. At least one woman in each subtype received some instruction from a career criminal, but there is no indication that these women had been accorded recognition as professional thieves or had enjoyed the benefits of a "group way of life" that provides unity and reciprocity. The majority of the women in this sample had no known association with professional thieves and had none of their identifying characteristics, except the innate or acquired attributes necessary to perform the crimes committed.

## The Career Criminal

A "career criminal" is usually considered to be a person who: obtains his entire livelihood or deliberately supplements a legitimate income through "crimes of gain, mostly property crimes"(15); incorporates in his life organization "roles built around criminal activities . . ., a conception of the self as a criminal and extensive association with other criminals"(16); continually strives to improve his ability to use the special skills and techniques needed in a particular kind of property offense(17); and commits his offenses in accordance with plans that reflect his perception of situations that provide maximum opportunities for success, and "are not the result of personal conflicts and immediate circumstances."(18)

None of the women included in this sample wholly meets the criteria established for this category. All the Reluctant Offenders and a high percentage of the Vindictive Self-Servers were motivated by "personal conflicts and immediate circumstances," and not by any planned effort to further a criminal career. (One woman may constitute a notable exception because deep-seated rage appeared to be propelling her toward a career of crime.)

Most of the women who intended to defraud were, at the time of their arrest, dependent in whole or in part upon crimes of gain for their livelihood. With one exception, the Vindictive Self-Servers gave no other evidence of intent to pursue a criminal career. Most of these women were using the money or goods obtained illegally to supplement an adequate salary or another means of support.

For obvious reasons, the Asocial Entrepreneurs most closely resembled the descriptive profile of a career criminal, but many of these women did not meet all the criteria listed. Most variations occurred in regard to: the concept of specialization in a particular kind of property offense; self-perception as a criminal; or extensive association with other criminals. Those who engaged in the traditional pigeon-drop presented the closest approximation to the career stereotype. They did specialize in a particular type of offense and had developed considerable pride in their ability to use the skills and techniques required. They did not regard themselves as criminals, however, and there was no evidence that they had had any recent association with criminals.

Not all Asocial Entrepreneurs seemed destined to pursue a continuing career in crime. The credit card thief who managed a free trip around the world seemed to have no desire to engage in criminal activities after she had paid her penalty for the calculated risk she elected to take. It seemed doubtful that she had or ever would have any extensive association with criminals. A few others with the knowledge and skills needed in legitimate employment may become "occasional property offenders" rather than career criminals.

## The Occasional Property Offender

As indicated in Chapter 2, many criminologists have included in their typologies one or more categories or subtypes designed to differentiate the behavior of a career criminal or "chronic offender" from that of the "occasional offender," the "situational offender," or the "one-time loser." When use of the concept is limited to property offenses, the occasional offender is generally considered to be a person who: commits one or more crimes against property but does not violate the law at frequent intervals; does not depend upon criminal activities for his livelihood or incorporate them into his life organization; does not perceive of himself as a criminal or associate with known criminals; does not acquire any special techniques for use in criminal activity; usually commits a crime only when he feels impelled to obtain or retain something he considers necessary and important but not available through legitimate channels(19); and may react with serious emotional disturbance when apprehended(20) unless he is able to formulate some rationalization that enables him to justify to himself his criminal behavior.

Without belaboring the point, it seems obvious that some women who intended to defraud could be classified as "occasional property offenders." Most of the Vindictive Self-Servers had no prior arrest record, had other means of support, and did not associate with criminals or perceive of themselves as criminals. Some variation from the definition seems apparent, however, because their criminal activity was usually motivated, in part at least, by some need for emotional satisfaction in addition to, or instead of, financial gain. Most Asocial Entrepreneurs seemed more likely to pursue a life of crime than would a true "occasional property offender." Nevertheless, the world traveler could probably be classified as a "one-time loser" property offender.(21) Others interspersed their illegal activity with legitimate employment, but seemed to have no qualms about illegally obtaining the things they considered "necessary and important" whenever these items (such as travel or comfortable living) were not readily available through legitimate channels.

In their original description of the "occasional criminal," Lombroso and Ferrero cited as examples of this type the women for whom, in many cases, "the origin of her reluctant crime . . . is suggestion on the part of a lover, or sometimes her father or brother."(22) Despite this fact, there would seem to be some question as to whether the Reluctant Offenders identified in this sample meet the contemporary criteria for classification as "occasional property offenders," especially in regard to other available means of livelihood, a life organization that does not include criminal activity, and no association with known criminals. In most instances, these women probably will not be able to withstand the demands of their husbands or lovers and will become habitual rather than occasional property offenders.

## The Naive Check Forger

Clinard and Quinney include in their description of "occasional property criminal behavior" the characteristics of the "naive check forger," who was identified by Lemert in his early study of forgery.(23) Because a high proportion of the women who intended to defraud used forgery as a means of achieving their objective, separate examinations of Lemert's findings and conclusions seem warranted.

Lemert designated as a "naive check forger" the person who usually: had "no other previous criminal record or previous contact or interaction with delinquents and criminals"(24); was socially isolated because of some dislocation in his situation or interpersonal relationships(25); had been faced with some imperative need for money; had perceived forgery as the only possible method of obtaining the funds needed; was impelled to select this method of terminating a tension-producing situation even though it did represent "behavior that was out of character and 'other than usual' for him"(26); and was able to justify his behavior and retain his self-image as a noncriminal through some rationalization based on the pressing nature of his need or the lack of injury suffered by his victim (for example, "the store makes a lot of money"). In Lemert's words:

> The hypothesis in general is that naive check forgery arises at a critical point in a process of isolation, out of certain types of social situations, and is made possible by the closure or construction of behavior alternatives subjectively held as available to the forger.(27)

Lemert's findings indicated that the usual "naive check forger" was a white male of superior intelligence who tended to be older than most offenders, to come from a good family, and to have achieved some competence in the professional, clerical, and skilled occupations.(28) It is therefore not surprising to find that none of the women who obtained other people's money through forgery of checks, money orders, or credit cards met Lemert's criteria for classification as a "naive check forger." In contrast, the women convicted on charges involving forgery included the two youngest members of this sample (22 years of age), and the total group tended to be younger (age range of 22 to 37 years) than other women who intended to defraud. None of the forgers had ever been gainfully employed for more than brief periods of time, and none had prepared herself for such employment. Some of these women did come from intact professional families, but there was no evidence that they felt any disruption of their relationship with the men who pressured or enticed them into forgery.

Approximately 60 percent of the women convicted on forgery charges were classified as Reluctant Offenders. Obviously, these women could not qualify as "naive check forgers" or naive forgers of credit cards because they had husbands or lovers who were pursuing criminal careers. More importantly, they had not been subjected to any tension-producing courses of action not related to their own criminal activity. A few women did express relief at their arrest and thus conformed in one respect to the behavior of some men in Lemert's study.

None of the Asocial Entrepreneurs who forged checks or credit cards appeared to have any imperative need for money beyond their own self-indulgent desires. There is no evidence that any of these women were socially isolated or had become involved in any course of action that would generate a thrust for its termination. The Vindictive Self-Servers who forged credit cards showed the greatest congruence with Lemert's classification. In most instances they had no prior criminal record or contact with criminals, and they were lonely and unhappy in their current life-style. However, they had not been engaged in any course of action that presented a critical need for money. Instead, they seemed impelled to use their arrests as a means of calling attention to themselves and creating embarrassment for significant persons in their lives. In this regard their behavior is not atypical; some men in Lemert's study also used checks as an act of aggression against a particular person or as a way of punishing persons in a primary relationship.(29)

The Systematic Check Forger

In his study of persons serving prison sentences for check forgery, Lemert classified as "systematic forgers" those who:

> (1) thought of themselves as check men; (2) had worked out or regularly employed a special technique of passing checks; (3) had more or less organized their lives around the exigencies or imperatives of living by means of fraudulent checks.(30)

None of the women classified as Vindictive Self-Servers or Asocial Entrepreneurs met any of Lemert's criteria as stated or when modified to include credit card forgery. Even the Reluctant Offenders who were involved in forgery did not meet Lemert's criteria fully. For two years prior to her initial arrest, one woman seemed to do so. Like some men in Lemert's sample she was not an isolate, but apparently limited her criminal association to "one other person upon whom . . . [she] feels . . . [she] can rely with implicit confidence"(31) – for example, her husband.

In brief, the Reluctant Offenders provided interesting data about women convicted on two or more occasions on charges involving forgery. Their assigned roles and their criminal associations, however, preclude their classification as "systematic forgers" or as "naive forgers."

## SUMMARY AND CONCLUSIONS

The data collected in this study identified three types of women who intended to steal or defraud. To paraphrase Conklin's findings in his study of robbery, each type of offender had a different reason for appropriating other people's money or property and a different degree of commitment to crime.(32) Unlike Conklin's men, however, the women in each subtype did not use comparable techniques to achieve their objectives. Instead, their modes of operation seemed wholly unrelated to their reasons for committing a property offense, to their life organization, or to the degree to which it involved a commitment to crime. Only the Asocial Entrepreneurs appeared to be their own women. They freely elected to undertake one or more criminal ventures, planned independently or with a trusted business partner the way in which a particular enterprise would be conducted, knew that any illegal activity involved a considerable degree of risk-taking, but optimistically believed that their wits and skills would bring continued success.

The Vindictive Self-Servers shared some of these characteristics in terms of independent planning, but seemed caught in webs of emotion that stemmed from unfulfilled dreams, unrewarding relationships with others, and perhaps some of the "need for closure" Lemert found in his "naive check forgers."

Like the Vindictive Self-Servers, the Reluctant Offenders were other-directed. However, their criminal activities were not planned by them and their primary motivation appeared to be a desire to please a husband or lover, or to avoid the abuse automatically following any refusal to comply with the demands of the men to whom they had attached themselves.

Further study will be needed to validate the impressions given by the data collected in this study, but it would appear that the behavior systems of the women who intended to steal or defraud were built around keystones formed by their self-perceptions, the quality of their past and current primary relationships, their attitude toward the larger society, and, to some extent, the nature of their current value systems. None of the typologies evolved from studies of male property offenders appears wholly applicable to women included in this study. It therefore seems important to determine whether the typology suggested in Chapter 8 would have value in predicting the probability of future law violation and possible means of preventing such violation.

## NOTES

(1) Edwin H. Sutherland, The Professional Thief (Chicago: University of Chicago Press, 1937), pp. 197-229.

(2) Ibid., p. 197.

(3) Ibid., p. 198.
(4) Ibid., p. 200.
(5) Herbert A. Bloch and Gilbert Geis, Man, Crime and Society (New York: Random House, 1962), p. 199.
(6) Sutherland, Professional Thief, pp. 202-3.
(7) Ibid., p. 204.
(8) Ibid., p. 207.
(9) Ibid., p. 209.
(10) Ibid.
(11) Ibid., p. 208.
(12) Ibid., p. 209.
(13) Ibid., p. 210.
(14) Ibid., p. 211.
(15) Marshall B. Clinard and Richard Quinney, Criminal Behavior Systems: A Typology, 2d ed. (New York: Holt, Rinehart and Winston, 1973), p. 131.
(16) Ibid.
(17) Ibid.
(18) Ibid.
(19) Ibid., pp. 60-75.
(20) Ruth Shonle Cavan, Criminology (New York: Crowell, 1938), p. 192.
(21) Don C. Gibbons, Society, Crime and Criminal Careers (Englewood Cliffs, N.J.: Prentice-Hall, 1973), pp. 320-22.
(22) Cesare Lombroso and William Ferrero, The Female Offender (New York: Appleton, 1900), p. 196.
(23) Edwin M. Lemert, "An Isolation and Closure Theory of Naive Check Forgery," Journal of Criminal Law, Criminology and Police Science 44 (September-October 1953): 304-5.
(24) Ibid., p. 277.
(25) Ibid.
(26) Ibid., p. 300.
(27) Ibid., p. 298.
(28) Ibid., p. 299.
(29) Ibid., p. 307.
(30) Edwin M. Lemert, "The Behavior of the Systematic Check Forger," Social Problems 6 (Fall 1958): 141.
(31) Ibid., p. 146.
(32) John E. Conklin, Robbery and the Criminal Justice System (New York: Lippincott, 1972), p. 182.

# IV

# WOMEN WHO PREVIOUSLY COMMITTED DRUG-RELATED OFFENSES

# 10

# SELECTED CASE STUDIES

The case studies in this chapter were compiled from institutional records. As a result, data about the women's education, attitudes, self-perceptions, life-styles, and relations with others are often lacking. The limited information on these and other women in this sample provides the basis for discussion in Chapter 11.

All women in this group had been sentenced to the California Institution for Women on charges of forgery. They also had in common long histories of recurrent convictions on a multiplicity of charges that included the sale or possession of narcotics.

## SUE

Sue, aged 24, was the youngest of 11 children born into a very poor family. She had limited intellectual capacity (I.Q. of 89) and was first arrested at the age of 13. Soon after this, she dropped out of school because of pregnancy. At the time of her commitment fo CIW, one brother was in a state hospital.

Between the ages of 13 and 21, Sue became the mother of two more children and acquired a narcotics dependency. Little is known of her life during this period, but there is no evidence that she was ever legally employed.

Sue's first major offense was grand theft. She broke into a locked automobile and stole a gun, luggage, a transistor radio, various items of identification, and a checkbook. She received a jail sentence on charges of theft and addiction.

Two years before her commitment to CIW, Sue entered into a common-law relationship. One evening her lover's brother appeared at their apartment. Other friends soon gathered, and in a sudden quarrel the brother was stabbed and died almost instantly. Sue and three codefendants were charged with voluntary manslaughter. Sue was also charged with forgery of five stolen checks and with the use and sale of narcotics. She explained in a matter-of-fact way that the money she obtained through forgery was needed to support her heavy heroin habit.

## MARY

Mary, the second of three children, had a lonely and tragic childhood. Before the birth of her first chid, Mary's mother was hospitalized for mental illness and never fully regained her health. When Mary was ten years old, her three-year-old sister was killed in an automobile accident, and at some point her paternal grandmother and aunt committed suicide.

Mary's record showed an I.Q. of 124 but her educational achievement is unclear. It is known that she spent most of her time at an ice skating rink and began to believe that she could become a professional ice skater. When she felt ready to compete, she won a spot in the chorus of an ice show.

Despite her success, Mary began a series of criminal activities eight years before her commitment to CIW. Her first arrest occurred when she was charged with lewd and immoral behavior and with contributing to the sexual delinquency of a minor boy. She was placed on probation but allowed to retain her job with the ice show.

Two years later, Mary was jailed for conspiracy to commit forgery. In the following year she was charged with false identification to cash checks and with possesion of narcotics. One year later Mary was again jailed for being drunk in a public place. Two years elapsed before she and her husband were arrested for burglary and receiving stolen property. In the same year she was charged with misuse of a credit card. The following year she was jailed again for shoplifting and possession of heroin.

During this time Mary acquired two husbands, the first a drug pusher and the second a heroin addict who became her crime partner in efforts to support their heroin habits. At the time of her commitment to CIW, Mary had two children, one by each husband. A third child had been placed for adoption at an earlier date.

Mary and her current husband appeared to have developed two patterns of criminal behavior, both involving the illegal acquisition of auto parts. At first, they were successful in a series of efforts to burglarize garages and sell the auto parts they had stolen. They had received jail sentences for this activity two years before Mary was committed to CIW, but apparently resumed this modus operandi after their release. This method of obtaining money for heroin was interspersed with the theft and misuse of credit cards to obtain auto parts.

Mary was finally committed to CIW on three counts of credit card forgery and for receiving stolen goods. In this episode she first used a stolen credit card to buy $35 worth of auto parts, used the same credit card in another outlet to cover a purchase of $50 in auto parts, and the same card in a third store for the same kind of merchandise. She was arrested within hours of the transaction at the third store.

## DELLA

Della, the youngest of two children, had been a heroin addict since the age of 19. When she was 16, her father threatened to commit her to juvenile hall for truancy, using pills, smoking pot, and being "uncontrollable." Della responded by slashing her wrists in a serious effort to end her life. Her parents consequently relented, but both lost interest in her when they divorced and married new spouses.

After completing two years of high school, Della married a nonuser of narcotics who soon recognized that he was failing in his efforts to reform her. After two years of marriage, he divorced Della and received custody of their child.

Della continued to be totally lacking in any perception of the direction her life was taking. As her need for money to support her addiction became crucial, Della accumulated 12 arrests for petty theft, shoplifting, and drug possession. In the intervening months, she became increasingly convinced that she would not be able to support her drug needs by petty larceny. She solved her problem, for the time being, by marrying Don, a 30-year-old pusher who was using psychedelics. This chapter of her life ended dramatically a few months later when Don was committed to a state hospital for the criminally insane. After some 60 LSD trips, he had become too irrational and violent to remain in the community.

Della was now 28, alone again, and heavily addicted to heroin. She worked as a waitress and cocktail hostess but her earnings were not sufficient to support her habit. She turned to theft and forgery and was apprehended as she tried to cash a $200 check made out to another person. She claimed that the endorsed check had been given to her in payment for a car she sold the day before. When the identification cards of the check's owner were found in her purse, she was forced to admit that she had stolen this check by burglarizing an apartment in the building where she lived. She was then faced with the fact that she had cashed other checks she had made out to herself. These checks, she stated, were stolen by her addict-pusher friends and given to her. Della's assignment was to "move the paper" in return for narcotics and a small percentage of the money derived from the forgeries.

When committed to CIW, Della had compiled an arrest record that included six arrests for petty theft, shoplifting, and forgery and seven arrests on drug-related charges. CIW staff believed she had no interest in job training and no motivation to effect any change in herself or her life-style.

## MARIE

At the time of her incarceration, Marie was 26 years old and had had one legal marriage, two common-law relationships, and two children. Little is known about Marie's parental family except that she was the older of two children and that she perceived her mother as unfeeling and "cold." Marie was very obese. Before she was 15 she was taking an inordinate number of amphetamines (500 to 600 bennies per day) to control her weight.

Marie's first arrest occurred in a southwestern state. She was charged with the theft and misuse of a Chicago credit card. Those charges were dropped, but her record showed that she was subsequently arrested for prostitution, disorderly conduct, petty theft, and shoplifting, for which she served short jail sentences. During this period Marie worked for two months as a nurse's aide and for one week as a clerk in a doughnut shop. At other times she received public assistance.

At some time in her disorganized life Marie acquired an expensive heroin habit. To support her habit she stole blank checks, a grocery chain check-cashing card, and a hospital health card. She then forged and cashed checks for several thousand dollars, using the identification cards to establish her credibility. She also began to steal welfare checks from mailboxes, alter the checks, forge the signature of the legal recipient, and cash them. She found that altering and forging welfare checks was relatively easy as they were cashed without question. When arrested, Marie had stolen, altered, forged, and cashed $3,000 in welfare checks. She was apprehended when a woman, for whom she worked briefly, reported the loss of a credit card that she suspected Marie had taken. As her defense, Marie claimed the woman owed her back wages. This encounter with the police led to Marie's identification as the forger for whom the authorities had been searching. Because public funds were involved, Marie was committed to CIW on two counts of forgery despite the fact that this was her first felony conviction.

Marie readily admitted her addiction but did not use her habit as the reason for her criminal activities. Instead, she stated that she had tried to help herself and had stopped applying for General Relief even though she was destitute. Throughout her criminal history Marie was described as a loner with no crime partners.

## PEG

Peg, aged 31, had 17 prior arrests but was legally considered a first termer because her commitment to CIW was her first sentence to a state correctional institution.

Peg was the second of six children. After her mother died in childbirth, Peg and one brother first lived with their maternal grandparents and later with their father. Peg had a potential for educational achievement (I.Q. of 105) and seemed to be the only member of her family who was criminally oriented. Nothing is known of her adolescent years, but her adult record of arrests seemed to have little meaning to her. She was still surprised that she had been sent to prison for "the little things" she had done. She had only taken and fought for the things she wanted and felt she had a right to have.

Peg never married but had several brief common-law relationships. She had no children. Peg might be called "arrest and accident prone." In a nine-year period, these arrests led to probation: disorderly conduct, fighting, prostitution, fraud, vagabondage (twice in one year), shoplifting, battery, forgery (twice in one year), and heroin possession. In the next two years she was again arrested on a forgery charge and later on another shoplifting charge. In the following year she was arrested five times: first for heroin possession, then battery, later for shoplifting on two occasions, and finally for burglary.

Peg was committed to CIW after she was found in possession of 26 blank money orders that had been stolen from a liquor store. Because there was no evidence of forced entry into the store, it was assumed that the theft took place during normal business hours. Peg had previously cashed one $50 money order made out in her own name. Two days later she attempted to cash another money order for $100.50. Because the bank had been alerted to the stolen money order, Peg was quickly apprehended and convicted on two counts of forgery.

## PAM

Pam was 34 years old when committed to CIW on charges of forgery of checks and credit cards. Little is known about her background beyond the fact that she was an adopted child, had normal intelligence (I.Q. of 106), and had contracted two marriages from which five children were born. The record did not indicate the whereabouts of her children, but it was evident that she was not living with them at the time of her last arrest.

Pam's criminal activities began at an early age. When 17, she was arrested on a charge of endangering a child. In the following year she was charged with violation of probation by again endangering a child. It is probable that she served a jail term for these offenses, but her whereabouts for the next 13 years are not recorded. The record does show that she was a nomadic cocktail waitress and was also employed in factories at times.

When 28 years of age, Pam embarked on a new criminal career in which she used many aliases. She was first arrested for possession of heroin and, six months later, for forgery. In the following year there were two separate convictions on charges of burglary and credit card forgery. When she was again convicted on forgery charges, she was committed to CIW.

At the time of her last arrest, Pam was living with a couple who became involved in her latest forgery efforts when she appropriated 200 blank checks they had ordered from their bank. Pam claimed she needed money to pay bills and that her friends had told her she "could use the checks." She was apprehended, however, on charges that she had used two stolen credit cards to make fraudulent purchases totaling $2,300. When arrested, it was discovered that she was driving a stolen car and had two sets of license plates for it.

Pam's psychiatric assessment in the institution described her as a "typical anti-social personality with no guilt feelings."

## IONE

Ione (I.Q. of 107) was the second of three children. Her father was a sheriff in a small county in the East, but little is known of her education or the reasons for her nomadic life. Her work history indicated that she had attempted to work at legitimate jobs but moved from one job and place to another. She had been employed as a bus driver, a bartender, a casino croupier, a butcher, and a camp counselor with retarded children.

Ione's criminal history was even more diversified than her employment record. Her file listed 20 arrests within a period of 13 years. These included two shoplifting charges, two motor vehicle violations, one charge of destruction of private property, four arrests for interception of mail for the purpose of forgery, three convictions for forgery, two for fraud to obtain prescription narcotics, two for transvestism, one for possession of marijuana, and one for possession of heroin.

Her first four arrests (three in one year) resulted in jail sentences on charges of larceny, misconduct in a motor vehicle, destruction of private property, and shoplifting. Four years later she was sent to a federal correctional institution for mail theft and fraudulent endorsement of checks.

She served several years, was paroled, and subsequently was returned for parole violation after she gave to another parolee a credit card that had been mailed to her. After seven months she was again paroled.

Nine years after her first arrest, Ione was charged with possession of marijuana. In the same year she was convicted on charges of fraud to obtain drugs, forgery of a prescription, and interruption of mail. She was finally committed to CIW on three counts of forgery after she obtained a supply of bogus checks, made them out to herself, and used her own identification. She cashed the first check for $160 at a liquor store and returned to the same store a few days later to cash another check. Two days later she returned and was arrested as she presented another bogus cashier's check to the clerk.

At the time of her last incarceration, Ione was 35 years of age, had never married, and had no children. Throughout her criminal activities she seemed to have had no crime partner. The person from whom she purchased the bogus cashier's checks was the closest approximation of an accomplice, but he was merely a broker with whom she had no continuing relationship. She was, in effect, a loner, with no close peers sharing her life, her drugs, or her money.

## NELL

Nell, aged 22, was the third of five children. She claimed that her mother showed love for her only when she was in trouble and that her father hated her and beat her. Nell was married when 15 years old and subsequently divorced. The child born of this union has been cared for by Nell's parents. Nell's educational achievement was not recorded, but tests showed an I.Q. of 115.

By the time Nell was 18 years old she had become addicted to dangerous drugs and had become so despondent that she attempted suicide. She was then sent to a youth correctional facility on charges of using dangerous drugs and leading a dissolute life.

When Nell was released on parole, a friend gave her six blank money orders totaling $600 and advised her to pick a name out of the telephone book as the owner of the money orders. She succeeded in cashing all the money orders but was apprehended when their theft was reported and the woman whose name had been selected was contacted by the police. Because her parents promised to make restitution, Nell was placed on probation.

While on probation, Nell was arrested on charges involving drugs, liquor, lesbian activities, and delinquent associates. These charges were dismissed, but six days later she was charged with grand theft, auto. This, too, was dismissed. After three months, she was again arrested and convicted of fraud and possession of illegally completed checks. This conviction resulted in commitment to CIW.

# 11

# FORGERY AND PREVIOUS DRUG-RELATED OFFENSES

Like all women included in this study, the women described in this chapter had been convicted on property offense charges and were currently serving sentences at the California Institution for Women. In contrast to the "honest" women who violated positions of trust, all women in this category had prior arrest records. They also shared these experiences: their prior arrests had resulted in one or more convictions on drug-related charges; and their current sentences were based on charges that included forgery of checks, money orders, or credit cards with no indication that these offenses were drug connected.

As previously explained, the women in this group were excluded from the sample of "women who intended to steal or defraud" because they tended to exhibit a unique constellation of behavior patterns, motivations, and personal characteristics. Further research may indicate that women previously convicted on drug-related charges should be considered a fourth subtype of women who deliberately acquire other people's money or goods. The data presented here would seem to require separate examination because the methodology used in their collection differed from that utilized in other parts of the study. Time did not permit interviews with the women in this group, and the data found in institutional records often failed to provide significant information about the offenders' attitudes, self-perceptions, life-styles, and relations with others. As a result, only limited conclusions can be drawn from these findings.

The sections that follow: describe the offense patterns evident in the arrest records of these women; present a somewhat incomplete profile of their characteristics and behavior; assess the degree to which concepts and categories developed in other studies seem applicable to these women; and conclude with a summary of the findings.

## TYPE OF OFFENSE

This phase of the study was designed to determine the validity of staff impressions that convictions on charges of credit card forgery and theft were bringing to CIW a new breed of property offender. It was subsequently discovered that many women selected by staff for inclusion in the sample had not been committed to CIW on charges involving credit cards. When women not previously convicted on drug-related charges were transferred to the sample of "women who intended to steal or defraud," it was found that a majority (62 percent) of the women previously convicted on drug-related charges had been sent to CIW on theft or forgery charges involving checks or money orders. In fact, only 50 percent of these women had prior convictions on charges of credit card abuse. Consequently, it seemed evident that judicial reaction to the relatively new crime of credit card forgery was not the common denominator that brought to CIW women with attitudes and behavior patterns different from those of other inmates. Instead, the primary factor appeared to be judicial intent to terminate, if possible, long histories of recurrent law violation.

With one exception, the women included in this sample had been convicted on forgery charges only when sentenced to CIW. (Atypically, Sue and her codefendants had been convicted on an additional manslaughter charge.) Except for their prior arrest records, the behavior of these women closely resembled that of the women with forgery convictions who were included in the sample of "women who intended to steal or defraud." Obviously, one difference was inherent in the criterion used for retention of women in the group described in this chapter – prior conviction for the sale or possession of narcotics. In any effort to develop a typology of women who commit property offenses, it seems important to consider that the variety and multiplicity of prior charges faced by these women appear to represent a significant corollary of their involvement in drug-related activities.

The institution's records did not provide a complete history of prior arrests and convictions because many of these women had been declared wards of the juvenile court in early adolescence, or had been placed on probation and subsequently returned to custody for reasons that may or may not have represented further law violations. Available data do indicate that: the number of prior convictions for each woman ranged from 5 to 20; more than 37 percent had been convicted of prior offenses on 13 to 20 occasions; and the prior convictions of the group had been based on a total of 22 different charges. In addition to those involving the sale or possession of drugs, these charges included: a variety of property offenses such as petty theft, shoplifting (75 percent of the women), forgery, fraud, and interruption of mail; and a mixed array of illegal behaviors, including prostitution (25 percent), transvestism (one woman), leading a lewd and immoral life, seduction of minor boys, endangering the life of a child, public drunkenness, assault and battery, vehicle violation, and voluntary manslaughter.

## COMPOSITE PROFILE: WOMEN WHO COMMIT FORGERY AN DRUG-RELATED OFFENSES

Because data customarily obtained through interviews (for example, appearance, attitudes, interpersonal relationships) were not available uniformly, it is not possible to provide a comprehensive or in-depth description of the women in this category. The following characteristics appeared evident from recorded information, supplemented by some discussion with the staff.

### Normal or Above-Average Intelligence

None of the women in this group reflected a high level of intelligence. The I.Q. range spanned from 89 to 124. However, all the women except one tested above 105.

### Less than 35 Years of Age

None of the women was older than 34 years of age when sentenced to CIW. The ages ranged from 22 to 34 years; 37 percent were under the age of 24.

### Limited Education

Educational data were incomplete, but it seemed doubtful that any woman had completed more than two years of high school. This assumption is based, in part, upon records indicating that a majority had dropped out of school between the ages of 13 and 16 because of pregnancy, drug abuse, or histories of juvenile offenses.

### Absence of Occupational Skills

None of these women appeared to have any education or training that would qualify them for future employment. One woman had received training as a professional ice skater, but her ability to resume this role seemed dubious.

### Lack of Stable Employment History

Employment data were not uniformly available, but there was no indication that any of these women had any history of sustained employ ment. About 37 percent had had brief experience as a cocktail waitress, restaurant waitress, hostess, R.N.'s assistant, or factory worker. One held a variety of jobs that included work as a meat cutter, bartender, bus driver, dealer in a casino, and aide in a facility for retarded children. The remaining women appeared to have had no legal employment.

### No Currently Existing Marriage

Less than 25 percent of the women in this sample had an intact marriage at the time of their last arrest. About 37 percent had never married.

Seventy-five percent of the women had from one to five children, but data about the children's care were sparse. In most instances, the children were not living with them at the time of their last arrest.

### Little Evidence of Responsible Role in Parental Family

Information about the parental families was not uniform, but the majority (52 percent) mentioned unsatisfactory relationships with one or both parents. Only one woman was a firstborn child, about 50 percent were second in birth order, and only 37 percent had more than two siblings.

### Early Involvement with Drugs or Delinquent Behavior

About 87 percent of the women had been apprehended for delinquent behavior between 13 and 18 years of age, and 25 percent began drug use at 15 to 16 years. One was pregnant at 13 and another married at the age of 15.

## THEORETICAL DIMENSIONS

In many ways, the behavior of the women in this group probably resembled that of the men excluded from Lemert's study of the "systematic check forger" – forgers for whom this offense was "simply an aspect of alcoholism, gambling, or one of a series of criminal offenses having little or no consistency."(1) Because men fitting this pattern were excluded from that study, their personal characteristics remain unknown. It is certain that the women described in this chapter did not display the characteristics Lemert identified in his final sample of systematic forgers; the offenses committed by these women were not limited to the passage of fraudulent checks and they had not organized their lives around this activity.(2) It is equally evident that the variety of their offenses and the multiplicity of their arrests would also disqualify them from Lemert's consideration as "naive check forgers."

Because we have no basis for comparison with male forgers with prior convictions on drug-related charges, there may be particular value in reviewing the limited data available from this study.

## Motivation

Institution records frequently failed to provide a clear indication of the immediate relation between drug addiction and the property offense behavior that resulted in commitment to CIW. This is true, in part, because current sentences were not based on drug-related charges. However, it is known that 50 percent of the women in this group freely admitted that they had committed forgery to support heroin habits costing hundreds of dollars a day.

It seems probable that the remaining women had also returned to drug use after prior incarceration, but the absence of any statement to this effect, and the nature and variety of charges listed in their arrest records, would seem to indicate generalized patterns of deviant behavior that may or may not have included drug use. As Peg stated, she had never felt she would go to prison for "the little things" she had done. Arrests on charges of disorderly conduct, prostitution, fraud, vagabondage, shoplifting, forgery, and assault and battery had preceded her first conviction for heroin possession. She had also been convicted of similar charges on five occasions since her last arrest for possession of heroin. As she explained, she had only taken things she wanted.

Recorded information indicates that a wide variety of human emotions may have motivated these women in beginning a life of criminal behavior – for example, adolescent battles of will with parents, sibling competition for parental attention and love, poverty and its attendant lack of resources equivalent to those of their peers, lack of interest in school, and influence of peers already immersed in deviant activities. It seemed apparent that initial precipitating factors lost their identities as recurrent patterns of behavior developed. The property offenses that resulted in commitment to CIW were wholly motivated by a felt need for money – for drugs, for basic survival, or for luxuries.

## Self-Perceptions and Value Systems

None of the women in this sample gave any indication that they considered themselves to be criminals. Those who admitted recent drug addiction seemed to perceive themselves as victims of some malevolent force and to expect understanding that their behavior was necessarily dictated by the need for funds to support their habit. The others seemed to have value systems characteristic of sociopaths. The psychiatric assessment of Pam's behavior and personality structure appeared equally applicable to most of the other women: "typical anti-social behavior; no guilt feelings; does not learn from experience; blames others."

## Commitment to Crime as a Way of Life

Because these women did not regard themselves as criminals, it seems probable that they had no conscious intent to pursue criminal careers. Nevertheless, there is little reason to believe that commitment to CIW would permanently interrupt their illegal activities. This assumption is based on three sets of data: the recorded duration of their arrest records, their employment records, and institutional staff reports that these women had no interest in skill training and no desire to modify their behavior or effect any changes in themselves.

As previously noted, official crime records do not include offenses committed as juveniles. Institutional files indicated, however, that at least 37 percent had committed delinquent acts that presumably brought them within the jurisdiction of a juvenile court. Their arrest records as adults extended over periods of 4 to 14 years. When these facts are considered, together with their limited education, their lack of job skills, and the absence of any motivation toward acquiring job training, it seems likely that most of the women would revert to illegal activities soon after their release from CIW. This would seem particularly true for those known to have had costly drug habits at the time of their arrest (50 percent).

## OTHER CLASSIFICATIONS AND TYPOLOGIES

In many ways, the offense records and behavior patterns of these women seemed to resemble most closely those of the "habitual offenders" described by Moreau, Reckless, and Cavan in previous decades. As noted in Chapter 2, Reckless excluded from consideration as career criminals "habitual drunkards, sex offenders, drug addicts . . . who have no specialized form of theft and . . . habitual offenders who are driven by strong mental components to repeat in crime and to relapse time after time."(3) Cavan amplified this concept by describing, as subtypes, drunkards, drug addicts, vagrants, petty thieves, and criminal vendors (small drug peddlers and semiprofessional prostitutes), and by noting that the offenses of the habitual criminal are "either habits in the literal sense of the word which have been made illegal, or they are crimes in the common acceptance of the term repeatedly but not skillfully performed."(4)

In any effort to utilize the more recent typology developed by Clinard and Quinney, it soon became apparent that the criminal behavior patterns of the women in this group could not be properly classified in any single category. Of the nine criminal behavior systems defined by these authors, at least three would seem applicable to one or more women in this group: "violent personal criminal behavior" (assault, battery, voluntary manslaughter); "public order criminal behavior" (prostitution, drunkenness, drug use, transvestism, traffic offenses); and "conventional criminal behavior" (larceny, burglary).(5) Therefore, the nature of the offense does not seem to provide a useful basis for examining the behavior of women who commit a constellation of offenses that include only two common charges: forgery and drug-related law violations.

None of the women in this group had ever been convicted of robbery. In some respects, however, their behavior resembled that of Conklin's "addict robber."(6) Like the men Conklin described, these women appeared to "engage in less planning than professionals prior to their crimes," to choose a target in such a way as to minimize risk, and to be "less likely than the professional to select a target which will net a large gain."(7) Like the "addict robbers," they may have been impelled by a desperation for funds with which to buy drugs – which, in turn, resulted in inadequate planning of their illegal activities, carelessness in selecting a victim or in executing the offense, and a tendency to be caught more often than a professional.(8)

Like that developed by Clinard and Quinney, Roebuck's typology includes three categories that bear some relationship to the characteristics and behavior of women previously convicted on drug-related offenses: the "drug addict," the "mixed pattern offender (jack-of-all-trades)," and the "others" (no pattern). The women in this group resembled Roebuck's addicts in that they were young and had average intelligence. However, unlike the men in his sample: their early adjustments in family, school, and community usually were not "favorable"; they did not seem to be "products of families that enjoyed strong ties"; a high majority had presented disciplinary problems at home and school; and most of them did have delinquent companions and juvenile court records.(9)

Their offense records indicated further similarities and differences. Multiple arrests were common to both groups, but a majority of Roebuck's addicts "had never been arrested prior to their first use of drugs," and a preponderance of their subsequent arrests were for violation of drug laws.(10) The property offenses committed by both groups were similar (shoplifting, thefts, burglaries), but the male addicts were rarely involved in sex offenses and other offenses against the person.(11) Their most significant differences might be found in the fact that half of these men had been gainfully employed as musicians in nightclubs, while the majority of the women had never had any legal employment.(12) From the meager information available, it would also appear that most of the women could not be described as "passive-dependent personality types" who had been reared and protected by dominant mothers.(13)

In many ways, the life experience and offense records of Roebuck's "mixed pattern offenders (jack-of-all-trades)" more closely resembled those of the women in this sample than did those of his "drug addicts." Both groups had: conflict within their families and weak parental ties; disciplinary problems at home and school; delinquent companions; and frequent police contacts before reaching the age of 18.(14) Both groups also lacked job skills and depended upon their criminal activities for economic support. However, their mental ability and self-perception seemed very different. With one exception, the women described here had normal intelligence, while the mean I.Q. of Roebuck's "mixed pattern offenders" was 85.8.(15) Both groups seemed naive in the ways of crime, but the men clearly regarded themselves as criminals and seemed frustrated because more successful criminals had not been willing to teach them or to incorporate them into their criminal activities.

In Roebuck's residual group, the men designated as the "no pattern type" shared some of the characteristics and self-concepts of the women described here. They were young, had normal intelligence, and did not consider themselves to be criminals. However, their offense records, life patterns, and motivation presented marked contrasts. None of these men had more than two arrests and nearly three-fourths had had a regular work history. With one exception they did not have delinquent companions before the age of 18 and had found their adult companions in a noncriminal society. Property offenses such as grand larceny and embezzlement had been committed by slightly more than one-half, but the other arrests had been on very different charges.(16) Nearly 50 percent of these men were considered "problem drinkers," and approximately 75 percent claimed to have been under the influence of alcohol when their crimes were committed. Unlike the women in this sample, "their criminal acts generally grew out of an immediate unplanned situation,"(17) which caused them to become "occasional, situational offenders."(18)

None of the subtypes described by Gibbons as "property offender careers" appears wholly applicable to the women in this group: the "semiprofessional property crime role career," the "amateur shoplifter role career," and the "naive check forger role career."(19) This is true, in part, because the multiplicity of offenses committed by these women makes it evident that none had pursued a single type of offense career or had developed even semiprofessional skill in criminal activity.

Lack of relevant data makes it difficult to compare with any degree of accuracy the attitudes, family backgrounds, or self-concepts of these women with the dimensions described by Gibbons in his definition of the "opiate addict role career."(20)

## SUMMARY AND CONCLUSIONS

This phase of the study was conducted at the request of institutional staff. Because of time limitations, pertinent data were secured from institution records and conferences with staff. Only limited conclusions can be drawn because data customarily obtained through interviews (appearance, attitudes, ability to relate to others) were not uniformly available, and institution records often failed to provide information about the offender's self-perception, life-style, primary relationships, and group associations.

Under existing circumstances, it did not seem possible to identify clearly any subtypes among the women who previously committed drug-related offenses. It is interesting to note that none of these women appeared to be "medical addicts" – that is, persons who became addicted through drugs legally prescribed to relieve pain. It is also evident that, with one possible exception (the ice skater), addiction did not develop as an occupational acculturation process similar to what occurs among some rock groups.

The data collected are more provocative than enlightening. Further research will be needed to determine whether women who commit forgery and drug-related offenses should be considered a separate type of property offender or, perhaps, a fourth subtype of "women who intended to steal or defraud."

## NOTES

(1) Edwin M. Lemert, "The Behavior of the Systematic Check Forger," Social Problems 6 (Fall 1958): 141.

(2) Ibid.

(3) Walter C. Reckless, The Crime Problem, 3d ed. (New York: Appleton-Century-Crofts, 1961), pp. 79-82.

(4) Ruth Shonle Cavan, Criminology (New York: Crowell, 1938), pp. 204-22.

(5) Marshall B. Clinard and Richard Quinney, Criminal Behavior Systems: A Typology, 2d ed. (New York: Holt, Rinehart and Winston, 1973), pp. 16-17.

(6) John E. Conklin, Robbery and the Criminal Justice System (New York: Lippincott, 1972), pp. 71-74.

(7) Ibid., p. 72.

(8) Ibid.

(9) Julian B. Roebuck, Criminal Typology (Springfield, Ill.: Charles C. Thomas, 1967), p. 120.

(10) Ibid., p. 123.

(11) Ibid., p. 118.

(12) Ibid., p. 123.

(13) Ibid., p. 126.

(14) Ibid., p. 173.

(15) Ibid.
(16) Ibid., pp. 220-24.
(17) Ibid., p. 221.
(18) Ibid., p. 220.
(19) Don C. Gibbons, Society, Crime and Criminal Careers (Englewood Cliffs, N.J.: Prentice-Hall, 1973), pp. 260-322.
(20) Ibid., pp. 430-35.

# V

# CONCLUSIONS

# 12

# TENTATIVE TYPOLOGY AND CONCLUSIONS

This study was initially designed to determine whether the conclusions presented by Cressey in Other People's Money are equally valid for women who misappropriated funds after accepting a position of trust in good faith.

As the study proceeded, it soon became apparent that the problems encountered by the men in Cressey's sample were essentially different from those motivating a violation of financial trust by women. More importantly, the nature of the problems the women attempted to solve through trust violation seemed to provide a nucleus for homogeneous systems of behavior. Out of this realization came the decision to attempt to develop a typology that could identify both the behavior systems common to the "honest" women who violated financial trust and those characteristics of women who intended to steal or defraud – that is, women who committed similar property offenses but did not meet the Cressey criteria.

The sections that follow will: summarize and present, as a single entity, the tentative typology described in earlier chapters; comment briefly on significant areas of difference in this and the Cressey study; and conclude with a brief summary.

## TENTATIVE TYPOLOGY: WOMEN WHO EMBEZZLE OR DEFRAUD

### "Honest" Women Who Violated Financial Trust

The results of this study seemed to identify four different systems of behavior among the women in this sample.

#### The Obsessive Protectors

The women in the Obsessive Protectors subgroup appeared to violate their own value systems and to consciously sacrifice their positions of trust in an effort to meet responsibilities associated with the role of wife and mother. Alternative methods of securing needed funds were sometimes rejected or not explored. None of these women appeared to have been exposed to any group definitions of situations in which crime is appropriate or to any experience with criminal ideology.

The Romantic Dreamers

Romantic Dreamers are not primarily concerned with the real needs of significant persons (such as a need for medical care). Instead, they sought to preserve what they considered their most important possession (a husband's love), or to enhance a relationship with a lover or relative. Like the Obsessive Protectors, these women had also been conditioned to believe that preservation of a relationship with a beloved person justified any necessary sacrifice of personal values or positions of trust. They, too, had had no contact with criminal ideology.

The Greedy Opportunists

Most Greedy Oportunists began their illegal activities to meet financial needs involving the welfare of significant persons or their relationship with such persons. After discovering the ease with which they could obtain other people's money, they became addicted to the good life. Some of these women seemed to "become criminals without intending to do so."

The Victims of Pressure or Persuasion

Women who were Victims of Pressure or Persuasion accepted positions of trust in good faith, but subsequently violated that trust in response to pressure exerted by another person. Like the Romantic Dreamers they were impelled to violate trust through fear of the loss of a significant person or belief that a satisfying relationship would be irreparably damaged if they did not comply with a request for funds or did not follow the example of another person with superior power.

In all instances, these women had held positions of trust for long periods of time (7 to 25 years) and had not taken any prior advantage of their opportunity to secure money illegally. They accepted full responsibility for devising ways to obtain money fraudulently and for implementing their plans. They had no crime partners even though other persons provided the motivation for their crimes.

## Women Who Intended to Steal or Defraud

Three behavior systems were identified among the women in this group.

## The Vindictive Self-Servers

Vindictive Self-Servers appeared to believe that: their life experience entitled them to some compensation for childhood deprivations or adult hardship; and that the acquisition of money or goods by illegal means is therefore a defensible act or method of earning a livelihood.

Although financial gain was an immediate objective, these women seemed impelled toward some action that would provide an emotional outlet for pent-up feelings of loneliness, envy, frustration, disillusionment, or self-pity. Their future criminal careers were not predictable because none of these women had any prior arrest record. In some instances, it seemed probable that their hostility and some prior association with the criminal world would propel them into fully developed criminal careers. In others, the crime committed might well represent a cry for help, an effort to punish significant persons, or a need for self-punishment.

## The Asocial Entrepreneurs

Asocial Entrepreneurs are women who: engaged in a wide variety of fraudulent activities; assumed full responsibility for planning and executing their illegal schemes or shared such responsibility with a coequal partner; and justified their criminal behavior by equating their activities with those of legitimate business entrepreneurs or by citing the larcenous desires of their victims.

These women seemed motivated primarily by a desire to acquire, through any means available, the creature comforts to which they aspired (good cars, travel, or comfortable living quarters). None of these women denied an intent to defraud or indicated any remorse. The majority seemed to identify themselves with a career criminal role, but there was no direct evidence of any association with criminals other than their crime partners, usually a husband, son, or female associate.

## The Reluctant Offenders

Reluctant Offenders had: committed various property offenses (forgery, credit card fraud, illegal possession of blank checks); assumed little or not responsibility for planning or initiating their criminal activities; and claimed that they were enticed or forced to engage in specified illegal acts by a husband or lover.

None of these women had a marketable skill that could produce legitimate income sufficient to meet the demands of their husbands or lovers. Approximately one-third seemed motivated by a desire to retain the love of their mates. The others appeared to respond primarily to threats or acts of violence. In most instances, the continuance of a criminal career seemed probable because there was no reason to believe they would be less influenced by a controlling male in the future.

### Women Who Previously Committed Drug-Related Offenses

The women who previously committed drug-related offenses shared: long histories of recurrent convictions on a multiplicity of charges that included the sale or possession of narcotics; and current sentences to CIW on charges of forgery.

The limited information available did not lend itself to the identification of subtypes among the women in this group. In fact, the manner in which they had insured survival seemed to result in a common behavior system that showed little variation in motivation, self-perception, or commitment to crime as a way of life.

None of these women appeared to have any legally marketable skills or any interest in acquiring such skills. A high proportion had been apprehended for delinquent behavior before reaching adulthood, and a significant number had begun drug use before the age of 16.

At least half of these women had committed forgery to support their drug dependency. The motivation of the others was less apparent, but the absence of any sustained source of support would indicate a dependence on criminal activities for survival.

## SIGNIFICANT AREAS OF DIFFERENCE

### Women and Men Who Violated Financial Trust

Unlike the men in Cressey's sample:

- Most of the women had not engaged in any prior activity that would cause them to be ashamed to share, with appropriate persons, their urgent need for additional funds. A few exceptions seemed to occur when a felt need for money related in some way to nonshareable behavior of husbands or relatives.
- Prior to their violation of trust, none of the women had encumbered funds, developed associations that demanded expenditures in excess of their legitimate earnings, or lost the approval of groups important to them.
- With one exception, the "honest" women made no use of the rationalization that they were merely "borrowing" other people's money. The woman who used this explanation initially replaced the money "borrowed," and then abandoned this justification when she realized the amounts she could repay would not meet the needs of her family.

- Most of the women were able to justify their behavior without resorting to the self-deception required by the "borrowing" rationalization because they had been culturally conditioned to believe that any conduct, including trust violation, is justified when it seems to offer the only available solution to financial problems that might jeopardize the welfare or cause the loss of a child or husband.
- Only the Greedy Opportunists appeared to have experienced a gradual erosion of values relating to honesty and trust and to have become criminals without intending to do so.
- A few Romantic Dreamers and Victims of Pressure or Persuasion appeared to be the only women who had any exposure to "group definitions of situations in which crime is appropriate."

In brief, the findings in this study seem to indicate that Cressey's hypothesis is applicable to these women only if it is modified to provide that positions of trust are violated only when the trusted person: encounters an urgent need for funds in excess of her legally acquired resources; realizes that her position of trust offers a solution to financial problems; and can formulate, in advance, a rationalization that will permit her to justify to herself a violation of financial trust without jeopardizing her self-conception as a trusted person.

## Women in This Study

Any attempt to compare the characteristics of the women who intended to steal or defraud with those of the "honest" women who violated financial trust reveals significant variations in motivation, self-perception, value systems, life organization, and commitment to crime as a way of life. It soon becomes evident, however, that meaningful generalizatins about these two categories cannot be formulated. Instead, it is necessary to examine separately the subtypes identified in each class and to determine, if possible, their similarities and differences.

The constellation of characteristics and behaviors shared by the "honest" women who recklessly sacrificed positions of trust to fulfill their preconceived roles as wives or mothers had no counterpart among the women who intended to steal or defraud. This dissimilarity appeared to stem primarily from the fact that most Vindictive Self-Servers and Asocial Entrepreneurs seemed intent on meeting their own needs rather than those of a child or spouse, and many of these women had no close relationships at the time of their arrest. Possible exceptions to these assumptions might be suggested, though it seems probable that Judy's alleged concern about the effect her continued prostitution might have on her son only served to provide a rationale for her decision to change the nature of her illegal activities. Conversely, Gloria's need to contribute to the support of her four children may have provided some incentive for the long series of legal and illegal business ventures she seemed impelled to undertake, even though her failure to use this rationale in her own defense would seem to indicate that concern about others played only a minor role.

The characteristics of women who violated positions of trust in response to some form of pressure from a significant person are in many ways similar to those of women who became Reluctant Offenders dominated by a husband or lover. In the small samples involved in this study, their basic differences appear to lie in the areas of self-perception and life organization. By definition, the women who met Cressey's criteria for inclusion in his study were qualified to hold positions of trust and for many years had fulfilled job responsibilities that involved the handling of other people's money. This may well account for the fact that all of these women accepted full responsibility for their illegal activity and seemed to have no need to project blame onto others. In contrast, most women classified as Reluctant Offenders in criminal activities planned by their husbands or lovers were dependent on the latter for support, had no marketable skills, and faced physical abuse as an alternative to compliance with the demands of the men in their lives. None of the "honest" women whose crime was induced by others had embraced a life-style based on criminal activities, but all the Reluctant Offenders were dependent emotionally or financially upon men committed to crime as a way of life.

Of the women who intended to steal or defraud, the greatest similarity among the three subtypes seemed to center around a system of values different from that of the "honest" women who violated financial trust. Further study will be needed to determine whether the emotional problems and life experiences of the Vindictive Self-Servers and Reluctant Offenders impelled them to abandon "previously accepted standards of behavior including an ideal of honesty,"(1) or whether they grew up in homes where "there was an early reliance on deceit as a major tool of life."(2) In any event, it seemed evident that, at the time of their arrest, the Asocial Entrepreneurs had little or no compunction about their efforts to obtain other people's money or goods fraudulently. Although the data are not conclusive, they tend to support an assumption that a strict code of honesty had never been a strong motivating factor in their behavior. It is possible, however, that for some of these women "a gradual modification of . . . values in regard to deceit, trust and honesty"(3) occurred as legitimate employment failed to meet their ever-increasing financial aspirations (for example, Josephine). From their histories it seemed evident that some women had "come into contact with cultural ideologies which sanction violation"(4) of commonly accepted standards of ethical behavior, while others had not become sufficiently acculturated to accept any standard that would tend to restrict their attempts to satisfy their own wants.

In some ways, the behavior of women who had previously committed drug-related offenses closely resembled that of the women with forgery convictions who were included in the sample of women who intended to steal or defraud. The most significant difference seemed to lie in the variety and multiplicity of prior charges faced by the women previously involved in drug-related activities. Like the Asocial Entrepreneurs, they seemed to feel little guilt about their appropriation of other people's money or goods. They did not see themselves as criminals. Instead, those who admitted recent addiction seemed to resemble the Vindictive Self-Servers in perceiving themselves as victims of a cruel fate.

## SUMMARY

The findings in this study substantiated a premise that typologies developed by other writers do not appear wholly applicable to women who illegally acquire other people's money. Consequently, a typology was developed, based on a study of incarcerated women who had been committed on property offense charges.

More extensive research is needed to determine whether the findings of this study can be considered valid for a larger group of women, including those in other state correctional institutions and those who received probation or a brief jail term on charges of fraud and embezzlement. The importance of extended research cannot be underestimated when it is recognized that ever-increasing numbers of women are finding opportunities for greater responsibilities in the corporate community, in other private enterprise, and in all levels of government.

## NOTES

(1) Donald R. Cressey, A Study in the Social Psychology of Embezzlement: Other People's Money (Glencoe, Ill.: Free Press, 1953), p. 142.

(2) Julian B. Roebuck, Criminal Typology (Springfield, Ill.: Charles C. Thomas, 1967), p. 185.

(3) Cressey, Other People's Money, p. 148.

(4) Ibid., p. 143.

# INDEX

# ABOUT THE AUTHOR

DOROTHY ZIETZ is Professor Emeritus, School of Social Work, California State University, Sacramento.

Dr. Zietz has done extensive research in criminology and social work. Her articles have appeared in Social Work, Prison World, California Youth Authority Quarterly, and Child Welfare.

Dr. Zietz holds a B.S. from the Illinois Institute for Technology, an MSW from Loyola University, Chicago, and a Ph.D. from the University of Maryland.

www.ingramcontent.com/pod-product-compliance
Ingram Content Group UK Ltd.
Pitfield, Milton Keynes, MK11 3LW, UK
UKHW020209290926
15470UKWH00001B/79

9 780275 907488